CLARIFYING ORGANIZATIONAL VALUES

Clarifying Organizational Values

Mike Woodcock
and
Dave Francis

Gower

Published by
Gower Publishing Company Limited,
Gower House,
Croft Road,
Aldershot
Hants GU11 3HR,
England

British Library Cataloguing in Publication Data
Woodcock, Mike
    Clarifying organizational values.
    1. Organizations.Objectives. Management
    aspects
    I. Title II. Francis, Dave
    658.4′012

ISBN 0–566–02822–0

Printed in Great Britain by
Billing & Sons Ltd, Worcester

Contents

Preface

This book argues that managers in successful commercial organizations hold roughly similar sets of values, and that successful managers have thought deeply about their own beliefs and aligned their organization's values to those described in this book.

A 'value' is a belief in action. It is a choice about what is good or bad, important or unimportant. Values shape behaviour. Until a value is acted upon it remains an aspiration.

Values are hard to detect. They underpin organizations like the foundations of a house. If the foundation is weak then the house falls down.

Every organization has a system of values whether it is realized or not. The most important value systems are located in the management group, especially at the top. Those who occupy directing roles must have an active value system – this is what top leadership is all about. In practice the principle extends right down the hierarchy; all managers make decisions of principle which profoundly influence the part of the community which they govern.

From this point of view management is a form of politics – the use of power in pursuit of collective aims. Managers establish systems for law-making, investment, justice, motivation, defence and so on. The way that this power is used defines the historical and cultural identity of organizations.

Those who shape the destiny of organizations usually have strong personalities and their views really matter. What do these people believe in? In this book we try to answer that vital question.

The book is a practical guide to value clarification for managers. It is intended for four audiences:

- managers who want to develop their own capability
- management teams who want to survey the values in their own organization
- personnel managers and consultants who design organization development programmes
- students of management who will, one day, be in positions of power.

This last category, students of management, deserves special mention. Very few courses for the Master of Business Administration degree contain a programme on values. It was not until 1987 that the Harvard Business School received a grant to establish a course which examines the ethical implications of management decision making. We believe that much more attention should be paid to the topic. Aspiring managers, who will shortly be in positions of power, need to have clarified their own values and thought about the implications of their stances on matters of principle.

We must be candid: there is no scientific process by which the ingredients for management success can be identified. Management is a 'craft' in the medieval sense of the word. It is based on beliefs which are implemented by instruction, practice, first-hand knowledge and close attention to detail.

To define the foundation of the craft of management we undertook a four-year study of interview, observation and 'measurement' using the Organizational Values Questionnaire which is reproduced later in this book. Sitting by the pool on Mike's farm (writing a book has its perks) we sifted through our observations and data to detect significant patterns.

First we needed a definition of success. For commercial organizations the task was relatively easy – sustained financial success is the only criterion which can be used. In non-commercial organizations the definition of success is more blurred. How do you measure the performance of a prison or a hospital? We took critical acclaim by informed observers as our criterion here.

Fortunately we were well placed to make the analysis. Our work enabled us to become 'participant observers'. As an MP, Mike Woodcock was a member of the Select Committee on Trade and Industry and had the opportunity to consider many case studies in Britain, parts of

Europe, Turkey and China. Dave Francis is a consultant on organization strategy and development. His close association with major
international companies provided much detailed observation of values
in action. Together we visited organizations in countries as far apart as
Sweden and Mexico, Spain and India, New Zealand and the USA.

As we debated the patterns which emerged from the data we were
struck by the similarity of managerial values across cultures – even in
the communist bloc. In commercial organizations those managements
that were successful, not surprisingly, had an almost total preoccupation with profitability. But there was another subtle theme which we
called 'the concern with legacy'. This meant that successful managers
were striving to build something worthwhile to pass on to the next
generation. These managers knew that mere wealth creation was
insufficient to inspire most people and sustain their hopes. They created
organizations with a heart as well as a pocket.

Successful non-commercial organizations replaced the ethic of profitability with a deeply understood, but continuously evolving, notion of
'contribution'. Their leaders had exhaustively examined the options
(including the needs of their environments) and had come to a firm
decision about their corporate identity. Managers in great hospitals,
theatres, prisons or universities know their mission with total clarity –
and it has a statement of the organization's contribution at the core.

Managers have often been cast in the role of harsh, reactionary
exploiters. Listening to those who hold such crude stereotyped views
one could be forgiven for believing that most managers are unenligh-
tened and uncaring individuals. This is often the opposite of the truth.
We found that, at its best, management is profound, positive, relevant
to today's needs and deeply humanitarian at its core.

So, in part, this is a book about management morality. The authors
do not pretend that management always equals good and we acknowledge that some managers have adopted exploitive, damaging and self-
aggrandizing strategies to the detriment of those whom they manage
and many others.

Successful managements establish what people really want and shape
an organization to fill a void. They provide opportunities for their
employees to thrive and develop. Management, at its best, is based on a
mature insight into what is, not an idealistic concept of what might be.

We devoted three years to completing this book which provides a
framework for managers, especially those near the top, to review their
organization's values in order that beneficial change may result. We

believe that successful managerial philosophies are based on fundamentally decent values, otherwise the right to manage is not earned.

In periods of rapid change or confusion people need a rock to stand on. This gives them confidence to enter the unknown and effectively manage change. A strong set of beliefs and values, shared by the management cadre, provides the necessary foundation for coping with difficulty. It is important that managers know the prevailing values which guide behaviour in their organizations and change those which are negative or destructive.

The topic of management culture has been much discussed, but the crucial importance of values has been insufficiently realized. Values in organizations are mainly established and maintained by leaders. Most people in organizations look to the top for definition of what is important. We need 'heroes' at the apex of organizations and 'mini-heroes' in all sections of the management structure. Values are essential whenever decisions are made, goals are set, or problems are solved. This is not moralistic: it happens anyway. Everyone in a position of power is well advised to clarify and test their values.

As authors we acknowledge a considerable debt to others who have analysed and discussed management sciences. In particular the work of Murray Smith on value clarification and Henry Mintzberg on organization have been great inspirations. There is, of course, no implication that either of these authors, or any of the other writers quoted in the text, agree with the thesis expressed here. Our chief debt, of course, is to the hundreds of managers who have answered our questions and helped us to clarify our thinking.

Mike Woodcock
Dave Francis

Introduction: The seven ages of management

A visitor to China went to see a prison on the outskirts of Canton. Entering the heavy gates of the stark building he expected to observe an oppressive regime with men incarcerated in almost medieval conditions. Exactly the opposite was the case. The prison was humming with purposeful activity. An orchestra of felons and murderers was practising a Mozart piece. Forgers and pimps were learning poetry. In every quarter there was a spirit of 'improvement'.

The visitor interviewed the prison governor who said: 'Our mission is to awaken the good in wrongdoers. This is not a prison in the accepted sense. We aim to be a true reformatory.'

A prison, like any other organization, is an institution built on a foundation of values. If the Canton prison governor had seen his task as merely custodial then everything would have been different. There would have been no indoctrination, culture or education. The emphasis would have been on constant surveillance and unpickable locks.

To repeat the Preface, values are beliefs about 'what is good or bad, important or unimportant'. Values beget attitudes which specify behaviour. The values of those who hold power determine the character of an organization.

Ideally all those who hold powerful roles within organizations share the same basic values. Think about the Chinese prison again. What would have happened if the prison governor had adopted enlightened values whilst the staff were repressive? There are three possibilities: the governor may succeed in changing the values of his staff, he may force compliance, or the staff might undermine the governor's power.

Since the effective power in organizations is spread across management, and sometimes wider, our researches clearly show that successful managements achieve a vital consensus on basic values.'(Our definition of 'success' was stated in the preface). Without a shared understanding of mission the organization is in peril of being figuratively, perhaps literally, torn apart. /

How is this consensus achieved? Values come from leaders. But there is a more subtle influence. Those in positions of power are influenced by the spirit of the times. Managers look outside themselves for guidance, whether they know it or not.

Values must be related to a particular context. Parents must look at the choices they make whilst rearing children, doctors must examine questions of medical ethics and managers must examine the specific issues related to the task of governing productive communities. Where do we begin our search for those managerial values which spell success?

In this introduction we follow the path the authors took when they began their study of managerial values. We will examine the development of management ideology in the twentieth century. Each era had something to offer. Assessment of the evolutions and revolutions in management values is a useful basis for our study. The introduction concludes by picking out the key themes of each phase and defining its . enduring value. As you read the next few pages see if you can detect the trends and try to assess which era of management values has affected your thinking the most.

Since the early days of management much has been written about the art and science of getting things done through people. There is an increasing number of sources of indoctrination which shape the minds of leaders. Autobiographies of management heroes adorn airport bookstalls and are avidly read in club class seats. New managers go to business school to learn their trade. Mass media are being used. For example, in Great Britain an increasing amount of management guidance is given on television through the 'Open Business School'. There is a whole industry devoted to satisfying the hunger of managers for inspiration and guidance. The effect of this 'propaganda' is partly to standardize managers' intellectual activity.

Why is this important? We believe that some influences on managers' values have actually undermined organizational effectiveness. Successful managers discriminate as to who they allow to influence them. In other words, managers are unwise if they unquestionably accept the viewpoints of today's pundits. Leaders must look past the fashions of the moment and answer the basic questions for themselves. Each era of management thinking has made a significant contribution. The lesson is obvious: managements must capture the best of each evolutionary phase and develop their own composite philosophy.

Management is a twentieth-century craft. When viewed from a historical perspective we see that there has been considerable change in the influences which have shaped the values of western managers. Only in the last ninety years has the role of 'manager' become distinct. Values have developed throughout this time. Although one could go into great detail it will be sufficient to describe the seven key evolutionary stages.

The first set of values to dominate management thinking was that man should be treated as a perfectible machine motivated by material gain. These values were based on concepts of organization which were first analysed about a hundred years ago. It was Max Weber who described the concepts of authority, hierarchy, roles, and formalized procedures. Such organizational devices enable human machines or 'bureaucracies' to be devised to perform complex but repetitive tasks.

In the first half of the twentieth century organizations became larger and overwhelmingly concerned with efficiency. Scientific thinking greatly accelerated the pace of change. Mass production methods changed the working lives of millions of people. Slowly the fruits of improved organization were harvested and material wellbeing improved.

It was found that people became more efficient when their work was carefully programmed. A new profession, work study engineering, developed. Men with clipboards and stop watches were soon to be seen observing workers and making changes in routines. The incremental effect was a massive improvement in productivity by use of meticulous analytical techniques which improved performance through careful experiment, specification of standards, and training. Most of the leadership advice of the time was based on values which assumed that men and women were a resource like any other; as machines motivated solely by money. The prevailing philosophy is best summed up in the writings of Frederick William Taylor, the 'father of work study' who advocated the obsessive pursuit of rationality in every aspect of life.

These techniques of mechanistic management allowed larger enterprises to be managed. Workers found themselves performing routine work alongside millions of others. But all was not well. New research studies (at the Hawthorne Plant in the USA) demonstrated that non-rational factors (feelings and attitudes) profoundly influenced behaviour and performance.

A second era of management values began. Progressive managers were forced to adopt a more complex view of the human being and to realize that feelings and will-power played a significant, sometimes crucial, role in influencing productivity. Many experiments took place to try to improve the individual's attitudes at work. Supervisors were trained to be team leaders and new techniques for motivation were tried. The new 'human relations school' refused to accept the assumptions of 'mechanistic' management, and there was much debate as to the right way to manage.

After the Second World War a new situation brought about a revolutionary change in the power structure of organizations. The third revolution in organizational values was not chosen by management – it was a response to the rise of trade union power. Management was forced to learn to fight. In the 1950s there was a huge shortage of products and labour; almost everything that could be made could be sold, so apparently there was little to be gained from being outstandingly creative or efficient. Trade unions gained in power because large organizations could be held to ransom by disruption by a few key workers. Values which had their roots in pre-industrial agricultural life – like diligence, opportunism, and a 'fair day's work for a fair day's pay – were often derided, especially in the older industrial nations like Britain.

Many managements invested enormous amounts of effort in warfare, containing unrest and peace keeping. The values of the era were adversarial, with shifts from confrontation to conciliation depending on management's view of the politics of the situation. It was questionable who was in charge of organizational values as active trade union leaders made so much of the running.

From the early 1960s, as the western world recovered from the shortages of war, many commercial companies encountered increasing difficulty in maintaining their profitability and market share. How could the problems of low efficiency, poor motivation, stagnant innovation and reactionary trade unionism be tackled? Various approaches were tried, including the disastrous philosophy of lowering the quality of the product. One country in particular seemed to be on a relentless downward spiral. Britain largely lost its commitment to the values which had made her strong. Ironically, people were perceived both as a valuable resource and the biggest barrier to change. Many managements came to believe that head-to-head confrontation was the worst available option and they sought new ways of solving the power problems. Slowly an answer appeared: democracy in the workplace.

Almost unnoticed, a fourth phase of managerial values became fashionable. The ideology of workplace democracy challenged long-held management beliefs. The boss was no longer the boss. A new armory of techniques was needed, and American influences began to play a dominant role. In 1960 Douglas McGregor published *The Human Side of Enterprise*, a book which was destined to have a profound impact on management thinking across the world. McGregor spelt out the importance of management value systems by dividing the beliefs into two opposite stances which he called Theory X and Theory Y. Theory X managers believe that people are naturally deceitful, lazy and not self-motivated – hence they need tight supervision and financial rewards. On the other hand, Theory Y managers see them as being naturally positive, trustworthy, altruistic and constructive. McGregor argued that these two stances were self-fulfilling prophecies: if you manage people from a Theory X viewpoint they will be unco-operative and deceitful, whereas people managed in a Theory Y regime are positive and self-motivated.

Many managers tried to develop a Theory Y style, but were unwilling to go the whole hog. One senior manager, reflecting on this era, said: 'we tried to trust people but never really took it seriously. So we diminished our Theory X behaviour and replaced it with a wishy-washy participative style which proved disastrous for all concerned.'

However, organizational idealism was in keeping with the mood of liberation and heady excitement of the 1960s. In almost every area of life people experimented with new ways of living, wanting to break the shackles of the past and plunge into the unknown. Everything was questioned. Authority was portrayed as outmoded and repressive. Remember 'Flower Power' and the Beatles song 'All you need is love'? These typified the spirit of the times.

This phase of the development of management ideology was most confusing. Supervisors whose task was to ensure that ten thousand switches were made each hour were enjoined to help the machine operators achieve a state of 'self-actualization'. Managers felt that they needed structure, predictability and performance but were told to be radical, libertarian and 'hang loose'. It could not last. The values of Californian hippies were unsuited to running productive enterprises.

The response was a new era of management values – the fifth. This was 'management by objectives'. Each person was meant to have comprehensive agreed output targets but allowed the freedom to determine the means of achievement. The aim was to harmonize the needs of the organization with the needs of the individual. Although the principle was sound managers found that MBO was only suitable in relatively stable environments and, even then, it bred red tape.

Managers became disenchanted with MBO and realized that the technique was not the organizational philosophers' stone. A new set of management values became current – the sixth phase. The managers of the 1970s increasingly turned to the mushrooming field of Applied Behavioural Science for their mentors. We saw the remarkable spectacle of senior managers sitting listening to gurus whose only expertise was radical psychotherapy. Many of the new authorities were American academics whose experience was gained in the sunrise industries like space science and high technology. Fads in management thinking emerged and managers began asking 'what is the flavour of the month?' Valid insights were gained, but with hindsight, it is easy to see that many managers tried to implement the fashionable new beliefs from a superficial understanding.

An analysis of the management propaganda of this era shows a distinct anti-authority bias in much of the guidance. The role of the manager was questioned and the concept of facilitator was advocated. Grand schemes for overhauling corporations were devised under the banner of 'organization development'. Managerial philosophers increasingly propounded a total 'social engineering' approach based on utopian humanistic values.

Many managements wanted to use progressive techniques and wholeheartedly embraced organization development. Top managers liked the notion that it is possible to change organizational culture and processes systematically. Enormous sums of money were spent in these heady years, but many schemes were later evaluated as failures. Few of the grandiose schemes survived into the 80s. Those which did have been carefully integrated into line management and outside experts, who used to rule the roost, have been relegated to their proper role as advisers.

Part of the organization development phase was an explosive growth of self-development activities. For example, experimental groups in self-understanding, known as T-groups, were widely practised. Managers were put in unstructured situations, often in remote locations, with a guru-like figure whose guidance was 'we shall learn from what happens'. Behavioural scientists had discovered that people learn much when the structures which support their present attitudes and perceptions are taken away. Many managers (over 50 per cent) reported that the T-group experience was profound and valuable, but an increasing awareness of negative psychological side effects contributed to such training techniques falling into disrepute. The aim was right: managers need to be aware of who they are and what impact they make on others. Unfortunately the techniques were often used by under-qualified trainers. One manager, reviewing this era, commented: 'Navel gazing replaced discipline and self-expression ruled the roost. It was a dangerous fashion.'

Self-development activities blossomed in the 1970s. The work of psychotherapists became fashionable. Perhaps the most influential was Eric Berne who developed an approach called Transactional Analysis which interpreted the exchanges (transactions) between people. Berne's work took managers on a fascinating voyage of self-discovery which related their insights to their management role. In particular, he helped many managers to see that they played destructive interpersonal games which sustained a negative emotional climate. Improved emotional health became an objective for many managers. Transactional Analysis brought alive truths in a way that no other popular approach to psychology had done but, for a moment, we shall examine the other side of the coin. Studying psychotherapies can result in a temptation to dilute self-expression with understanding.

For example, a drive for achievement can be interpreted as a manifestation of a neurotic personality. Creativity becomes expressed through human relationships rather than in the achievement of business objectives. As one observer noticed, 'the eye is taken off the ball when psychology becomes king'. A half-submerged assumption that people always ought to be nice to each other blunts the cut and thrust of debate. Interactions become games to be analysed preventing getting on with the job. There is no more irritating peson in management circles than a Transactional Analysis freak who is more concerned with expressing 'warm fuzzies' than achieving results.

Part of the sixth phase of the development of management thought was a growing concern with the quality of working life. Managers began analysing the dehumanizing and stressful aspects of organizational life. Fred Herzberg, an American professor, made a profound impact on the minds of managers in the 1970s. He probed into job satisfaction and motivation with refreshing candour, and concluded that material reward, supervision, and physical environment did little to provide motivation. There was a great need to build the opportunity for achievement into the very structure of the job. Unfortunately, it proved very difficult to find ways of enriching jobs to provide sustained challenge. People began to feel that they were 'entitled' to be satisfied at work. In some companies the efforts that management made to improve the quality of work life, ironically, provoked bitterness as it proved impossible to meet the early promises made to work people. The sense of detachment is summarized in a poem of the era entitled 'Work' (found on a cafe wall in Twickenham, England).

If you work and do your best
You'll get the sack like all the rest,
But if you laze and sod about
You'll live to see the job right out.
The work is hard, the pay is small
So take your time and sod them all.

The techniques we have mentioned, Organization Development, T-groups, Transactional Analysis, and Quality of Working Life programmes, are examples of the prevalent managerial values in the 1970s. The themes of involvement and participation were based on an underlying belief that people would support that in which they felt personally involved. Expectations were raised. Large numbers of people felt that they should not only participate in decisions, but also have the power of veto. Sometimes labyrinthine participatitive structures were established to provide those means of participation.

Despite the optimistic theories and brave experiments participation and involvement proved inadequate weapons in the fight against Far Eastern enterprise. Somehow those countries, like Japan, who had been written off as poor performers were overtaking those in the West. Harsh decisions had to be made, and the seventh phase of management thinking was rather brutally born.

This last phase in the development of management ideology is interesting because it was reactionary rather than 'progressive'. By the end of the 1970s managers began to rediscover lessons which their organizational grandparents knew well. Such themes as 'nothing is for free', 'hard work leads to success', and 'the customer is always right' began to be heard again. This was most obvious in Britain where the political stance of Margaret Thatcher's government, first elected in

1979, explicitly encouraged the virtues of Victorian values. Battles for power were fought against trade unions – with the establishment determined to win. The motivational power of individual opportunism, ownership and responsibility (all nineteenth-century values) were rediscovered. Attempts to democratize commercial organizations were largely reversed. State ownership was reduced in France, Japan, Great Britain and many other countries. Managements in the Western world moved towards the political right in step with the governments of the day.

The seventh phase in the development of managerial values is a synthesis of the previous stages. After decades of drifting managers have recognized their tough task of leading, controlling and winning. With global competition there are many more threats. Only the fittest will survive.

Successful values

Where do we look for the values which increase the probability that a management group will be successful? Your authors began with an analysis of the seven stages just outlined. They discovered the following key themes:

Stage	Theme	Enduring value
1st	Rationality	Scientific analysis pays
2nd	Emotionality	Care for people pays
3rd	Confrontation	Strong defence is vital
4th	Consensus	Politics matters
5th	Organization/Individual balance	Performance is king
6th	Potential	People can develop
7th	Realism	Nothing good comes easily

This analysis provided the basis for a practical study of managerial values. In Chapter 1 you will undertake a study of the values in your own organization. Only then, to avoid prejudicing your mind, shall we tell you the results of our research.

Part I

MAPPING ORGANIZATIONAL VALUES

1 Organizational values questionnaire

If you accept that values are the foundation of organization character then it follows that managers must strive to adopt a system of values which promotes success.

Now it's time for you to do some work! Before delving further into this book, take stock of the values which operate in your organization. This will relate the conceptual model of this book to your own situation.

In the following pages you will find the Organizational Values Questionnaire. This may be completed by one individual, or used as a survey of many people's views within an organization. However, the Organizational Values Questionnaire is used only with managerial, supervisory and professional staff.

Complete the questionnaire now. Instructions for interpretation follow.

Instructions

This questionnaire asks your opinions about a specific organization, or part of an organization. It may be a site, department, company, branch or a whole organization. Before you begin, define the unit that you wish to study and enter an unmistakable definition below. (When several people complete the survey together, ensure that all have an identical definition of the unit.)

> The unit being assessed is ....

Answer the sixty items below *only* in relation to this definition of the unit. Please give your opinion on each item. Even if you do not have enough information to make a definitive judgement, answer to the best of your knowledge. Allocate points as shown.

The statement is:

totally true	4 points
largely true	3 points
neither true nor false	2 points
largely untrue	1 points
totally untrue	0 points

Questionnaire

1 Managers act in ways which demonstrate that they are in charge. ☐

2 Much effort is invested in developing managers so that they achieve a high standard of competence. ☐

3 Outstanding managerial performance is well rewarded. ☐

4 Great care is taken to ensure that *key* management decisions are well considered. ☐

5 There is a constant search for ways to do things more efficiently. ☐

6 Managers avoid spending money unnecessarily. ☐

7 People with genuine difficulties are treated with compassion by management. ☐

8 Care is taken to ensure that everyone feels part of a team. ☐

9 Organizational rules and regulations are felt to be fair. ☐

10 The organization is aggressive in defence of its own interests. ☐

11 Everyone is aware of the importance of care for the customer. ☐

12 Innovation and creativity are encouraged. ☐

13 Management is respected. ☐

14 Considerable efforts are made to appoint the best candidates to management positions. ☐

15 Managers receive regular feedback on how they are performing. ☐

16 Over the past few years, the strategic decisions taken by top management have proved largely successful. ☐

17 New technologies and techniques are regularly investigated to see whether they would increase efficiency. ☐

18 Great efforts are made to ensure that people understand the economic contribution they are making. ☐

19 Employees are always given a fair hearing when disputes arise. ☐

20 Team-building techniques are used appropriately. ☐

21 Justice is done and seen to be done. ☐

22 Threats to the organization are treated seriously. ☐

23 This is an organization that believes in 'being competitive with the best'. ☐

24 New ideas are highly valued. ☐

25 Managers are widely perceived to have earned the authority which they exercise. ☐

26 Great efforts are made to develop the skills of managers. ☐

27 Managerial rewards are clearly linked to performance. ☐

28 Top managers plan well for the future. ☐

29 The organization is renowned for high quality goods or services. ☐

30 Managers are appraised on the cost-effectiveness of their units. ☐

31 Top managers demonstrate by their actions that they care about the wellbeing of the people in the organization. ☐

32   Employees strongly identify with their work unit.   ☐

33   Basic codes of conduct are well understood.   ☐

34   Trade unions do not undermine the wellbeing of the organization.   ☐

35   Competition between work groups is utilized to raise standards of performance.   ☐

36   The organization seizes opportunities as they occur.   ☐

37   Those with responsibilities are given commensurate authority.   ☐

38   People with management potential get real opportunities to develop their careers.   ☐

39   Performance is the main criterion by which managers are evaluated.   ☐

40   Top management decisions are communicated effectively.   ☐

41   Low standards are not tolerated in this organization.   ☐

42   Managers demonstrate by their actions that they understand the 'laws of the marketplace'.   ☐

43   This organization is considered to be a good employer.   ☐

44   This is an organization in which people go out of their way to be helpful to each other.   ☐

45   Internal rules and regulations are fair.   ☐

46   Management deals effectively with anything or anyone which could inhibit success.   ☐

47   Destructive competition between departments is avoided.   ☐

48   Entrepreneurial skills are highly valued.   ☐

49   Managers keep the organization, 'on course'.   ☐

50   The performance of managers is regularly evaluated.   ☐

51   People get rewarded for doing things which enable the organization to be successful.   ☐

52 Managers have been well trained in decision-making techniques. ☐

53 Pride in the job is demonstrated at all levels. ☐

54 Financial resources are used prudently. ☐

55 There are no destructive class or racial barriers in this organization. ☐

56 Deliberate steps are taken to develop effective teamwork throughout the organization. ☐

57 Rules help, rather than hinder, work accomplishment. ☐

58 Management fights to protect the organization's interests. ☐

59 Competitiveness in relation to other companies is regularly measured. ☐

60 Good ideas are acted upon quickly. ☐

Answer sheet

Write your score against each item number then total the horizontal columns.

Totals

1	13	25	37	49		*Power:* managers must manage
2	14	26	38	50		*Elitism:* 'cream at the top'
3	15	27	39	51		*Reward:* performance is king
4	16	28	40	52		*Effectiveness:* doing the right things
5	17	29	41	53		*Efficiency:* doing things right
6	18	30	42	54		*Economy:* no free lunches
7	19	31	43	55		*Fairness:* who cares wins
8	20	32	44	56		*Teamwork:* pulling together
9	21	33	45	57		*Law and order:* justice must prevail
10	22	34	46	58		*Defence:* know thine enemy
11	23	35	47	59		*Competitiveness:* survival of the fittest
12	24	36	48	60		*Opportunism:* who dares wins

Interpreting the questionnaire

You have completed the questionnaire and are, no doubt, wondering what it means.

You now have a score for each of the twelve managerial values identified on the righthand side of the answer sheet. High scores indicate a strong value, low scores suggest a weakness!

In Chapter 2 we show how the twelve values fit together into a comprehensive theory. Each of the subsequent chapters takes one value and describes its importance. We argue that a sound managerial value system requires *all* the twelve values to be strong.

Consider our arguments, evaluate whether you agree, and try the action ideas at the end of each chapter.

Copies of the Organizational Values Questionnaire are available from University Associates International Ltd, Challenge House, 45/47 Victoria Street, Mansfield, Notts NG18 5SU.

2 Twelve into four does go

The results of the Organizational Values Questionnaire (OVQ) will suggest which are the strong and weak values in your organization, but remember that one person's view is subjective and should not be acted upon without further verification. However, now you have completed the questionnaire you will find it easier to relate the theory of this book to your situation.

The answer sheet to the OVQ gives a score for twelve values which are vital for your commercial success. These are derived from four core issues and twelve sub-issues which have to be addressed by managers. The twelve values are those which are associated with successful management practice. The organizations which practise and hold these values will have the greater chance of success in today's world. In this chapter we define these values in outline and consider the process of clarifying values in an organization.

Our research and experience clearly points to a conclusion – that in today's world, if organizations are to be successful they must be able to:

1 *Manage management* – they must deal with the issues related to the power and role of management. They must ensure that the management role is clearly defined, and that managers are able people.
2 *Manage the task* – they must deal with the issues involved in getting the job done. Without results all commercial organizations will fail.
3 *Manage relationships* – they must deal with the issues of getting the best out of people. Organizations are about people; the job does not get done without commitment.

4   *Manage the environment* – they must deal with the issues of the competitive marketplace. They must know the environment in which they operate, and seek to influence it to their advantage.

Managing management, managing the task, managing relationships and managing the environment are the four core issues leading to twelve sub-issues and thence to the twelve values. These values have been derived from our research into those practices and beliefs which have shown themselves to be enduring in successful organizations. However, all organizations operate in environments which are, in some ways, unique. Additional issues may need to be addressed and other values formulated to suit a particular organization.

The four core issues, the twelve sub-issues and the twelve values form an integrated system. Their potential is realized when all are addressed with vigour and consistency. Our thesis is that the foundation of successful management is the active, almost obsessive, pursuit of *all* of the twelve values reviewed by the OVQ.

The first core issue: managing management

Almost every organization is complex, and specialist functions must be integrated for the organization to operate. Only management can direct and co-ordinate the complexity. Success requires that the management resource is well defined, well selected, well trained and well motivated. We call this 'managing management'.

There are three sub-issues.

Power

The management group should have the knowledge, authority and position to decide the mission of the enterprise, acquire resources and make decisions. Successful managements understand the inherent power of their position and take charge of the organization's destiny. They adopt the value: *managers must manage.*

Elitism

The management task is complex and important. The quality of people who fill management roles is crucial. An inadequate manager can wreak havoc – both sins of commission and sins of omission. Successful organizations understand the vital importance of getting the best candidates into management jobs, and continually developing their competence. They adopt the value: *cream at the top*.

Reward

The performance of those who lead organizations is crucial. Managers need to perform consistently and energetically in pursuit of the organization's goals. Successful organizations identify and reward success. They adopt the value: *performance is king*.

The second core issue: managing the task

Work can be dull, gruelling, demanding, challenging and worrying. But organizations are basically concerned with output, not the toughness of the task. The job must be done, and done well. This requires focusing on clear objectives, working efficiently, and not wasting resources. We call this 'managing the task'.

There are three sub-issues.

Effectiveness

Focusing on the right things must be a constant preoccupation. Unless effort is well directed, somewhere a smarter management will find ways of taking your market. Successful organizations are able to focus resources on activities which get results. They adopt the value: *do the right thing*.

Efficiency

It has been said that good management is about doing hundreds of little things well. All too often a small error makes an out-of-proportion effect on the quality of the whole. The drive to do everything well gives a sharp edge. Successful organizations relentlessly search for better ways to do things, and they constantly build pride in the job. They adopt the value: *do things right*.

Economy

It is a great deal easier to spend money than to make it. Lack of effective cost control is a common cause of business failure and organizational waste. The discipline of the profit and loss account gives commercial enterprises the ultimate measure of success. Every activity costs money; someone, somewhere has to pay. Successful organizations understand the importance of economic reality and that there is no such thing as a free lunch. They adopt the value: *no free lunches*.

The third core issue: managing relationships

Managers expect a lot from people who work in the organization. They want hard work, loyalty, skill, care and honesty. Such commitment will only be given to managements who are seen as being fit to govern. People need to be treated with compassion, feel valued, and believe that rules and regulations are just. We call this 'managing relationships'.
There are three sub-issues.

Fairness

One of the greatest compliments paid to a good teacher is that he or she is 'firm but fair'. Managements, by their actions, greatly affect people's lives, both in work and outside. What they do, and what they refuse to do, has a significant impact on the quality of life of their subordinates. The use of this power with compassion and fairness builds trust and commitment. Successful organizations realize that people's views, perceptions and feelings are important. They adopt the value: *who cares wins*.

Teamwork

A well-organized and motivated group can achieve more than the sum of the individuals who comprise it. People enjoy the company of others and can work well collectively. One person's talents balance the weaknesses of another. It is vitally important that people feel that they belong. Successful organizations ensure that they derive the benefits of effective teamwork. They adopt the value: *pulling together*.

Law and order

Every community develops a framework of laws which regulate conduct. These provide the ground rules of acceptable behaviour. Organizations exercise considerable power over the lives of employees and their families with managers operating as judge and jury, often without a right of appeal. Successful organizations devise and honourably administer an appropriate system of rules and regulations. They adopt the value: *justice must prevail*.

The fourth core issue: managing the environment

All organizations exist within an environment, sometimes turbulent, often hostile and complex. Managements must understand their environment from all viewpoints – social, technical, economic and competitive. Without this intelligence it is impossible to make wise decisions. In order to survive and succeed in their environment organizations must formulate a strategy of aggressive defence to protect their interests, take all necessary steps to be competitive, and seize opportunities whenever they occur. We call this 'managing the environment'.

There are three sub-issues.

Defence

For many organizations it is a dog-eat-dog world. In every commercial organization talented people are planning how to increase their business at the expense of the competition. Non-commercial organizations are often under threat from those who provide the funds. Successful organizations study external threats and formulate a strong defence. They adopt the value: *know thine enemy*.

Competitiveness

The capacity to be competitive is the only sure-fire recipe for survival. Usually, this truth is readily understood at the top level, but it is far harder for the message to be appreciated throughout the organization. Successful organizations take all necessary steps to be competitive. They know that in the world of commerce it is the best who survive, and the weakest who go to the wall. They adopt the value: *survival of the fittest*.

Opportunism

Despite the most brilliant planning it is inevitable that unexpected opportunities and threats will occur. Organizations cannot afford to ignore the unexpected. It is wiser to seek out new opportunities actively than to allow others, more fleet of foot, to grab the best chances. Opportunities often have to be seized quickly, even though this may involve risks. Successful organizations are committed opportunists. They adopt the value: *who dares wins*.

These are the foundations upon which organizational success rests. Each raises issues which need to be addressed. The twelve values, we conclude, encapsulate the characteristics of high-performing organizations in today's world.

Clarifying values

The twelve issues which determine success are shown in Figure 2.1. Our values, whether we are aware of it or not, determine our day-to-day behaviour. This is especially true for those in positions of power who must have clear and productive values. Management is weak and unfocused without a coherent value system. Power should always be used with wisdom and subtlety – domination will always be resisted.

Commitment management strives to do what is profitable but also what feels right. Values have to be known, consistent, practised and honoured. Values oriented to success need to be constantly re-enforced. There is no alternative. Leaders with clear values are able to attract others towards them, enabling the organization to develop a consensus about what is good or bad, important or not important.

Clarifying managerial values should be undertaken systematically. Much of the information comes from within the experience, beliefs and feelings of the senior management group. Value clarification is one of the few topics in management where inner beliefs are probably more important than external analysis.

A clarified value meets eight conditions.

1 *Values must be chosen from alternatives.* Only values that have been positively chosen will be firmly held. The act of choosing strengthens commitment.

   Senior management must debate issues of principle in order to choose those values they are prepared to fight to protect. For such

Figure 2.1 The issues wheel

debates to be meaningful managers need to consider each of the twelve issues described in this chapter. They are well advised to adopt a comparative approach and study successful and unsuccessful competitors to discover the values which have been shown to succeed in their own industry.

2 *Values must be consistent with each other.* Values must support each other. Values pulling in different directions are destructive.

For example, an entrepreneurial organization may adopt the strategic driving force 'we will not take risks'. This would be inherently contradictory, hence the message would be confused. Managers must study the package of values that they live by, and check that they are intellectually and behaviourally consistent.

3 *Values must be limited in number.* An excessive number of values dissipates effort and is confusing. Values are broad, deep and general.

The four core issues have been translated into twelve values to provide the framework for managerial policy making. Managers need to know the values of their organizations and then define the behavioural implications, so that everyone understands the relevance of the value to their own job.

4   *Values must be actionable.* A value that cannot be put into effect becomes a weakness: management should not be committed to an impossibility.

Top management should take great care not to incorporate pious hopes into its own values statements. All organizational values should be submitted to the 'for instance' test. Cases must be tested against the espoused value to see whether it holds up in all situations. Only when senior management is convinced that it can uphold the value in all eventualities should it be adopted.

5   *Values must be performance enhancing.* Values are an enabling device; they are a means of shaping an organization to achieve its performance objectives.

Value clarification is part of the development of corporate strategy. No statement of corporate strategy is complete unless it defines the wanted values – what is needed from people, and what is given in return. There must be a logical relationship between the key success factors of an industry and the values adopted by management. For example, an airline must be seen to be safe and helpful by its potential customers if it is to compete successfully. So values about 'doing things right' (efficiency) and 'who cares wins' (fairness) are crucial.

6   *Value must be attractive and 'pride giving'.* People should be uplifted by an organization's values. They should feel proud when playing their part in making performance objectives become a reality.

The values advocated by management must touch a deep chord within people at all levels. Values must be capable of being respected. People feel part of a greater whole when they can identify with the organization's goals. For example, airline workers can respect a preoccupation with safety from their managers: they only have to think of members of their own families flying on an unsafe plane to feel the importance of the value.

7   *Values must be capable of being communicated.* It is what managers do – symbolic communication – that is vital. Managers' actions must reinforce their value statements.

A key leadership task is translating values into terms that are meaningful to each individual. Managers should not adopt a value unless it is capable of being demonstrated. Managers must be the first group to adopt a value and from time to time they should collect data from below to see what messages their unconscious behaviour is communicating.

8   *Values must be written down.* Until a set of values is clear enough to be committed to paper it will not have the authority to be a leadership statement.

The act of writing down values has three benefits: it clarifies the mind; provokes debate and provides a message which can be communicated. It is the task of senior managers, those at the apex of the organization, to explore their own and their competitors' values and determine those that will provide the foundation for the organization's future. When the attempt is made to write them down, any logical flaws will appear!

How are these eight conditions put into effect? We have found that a sequence for value clarification is necessary.

Senior managers begin by reviewing the theory in this book and discussing the ideas. The aim is to see whether there is a will to go further. Then a formal decision to proceed must be taken. It is often helpful to appoint a task group to progress a values clarification project and organize the collection of data (using the OVQ).

A top team workshop may be conducted to determine the core values which should prevail in the organization. Confrontation and debate are essential to eliminate impractical values. The top team should determine the current values within the organization. The strategic plan should be reviewed to identify the values needed by the organization to achieve its goals. A written 'values statement' should be the final act.

Implementation policies should be devised which include communication strategies to cascade the message downward.[1] It is important to determine monitoring and control procedures to ensure that the programme is kept on track.

Management values are detected most clearly by looking at resource decisions. A small fortune spent on decorating the director's carport and nothing on the workers' squalid washroom says everything, no matter what pious statements are made.

Values tend to come from the top – but not always. The values of the doctors largely make a hospital. Trade unions shape some values. In

Vietnam the values of the soldier, the 'grunts', shaped the course of the war. Values which arise from below are sometimes productive; for example, a new top management may seek change without understanding the real competence of the organization. Those down the organization often have much insight into the real values which have inspired past success. The importance of honouring history is often underestimated by a thrusting young management team. Those ethics which enabled the organization to thrive almost always have merit. The future should conserve the best of the past.

The rest of this book consists of chapters on each of the twelve values. Each chapter is an essay which is meant to provoke reaction. As authors we do not want you always to agree with our views – we want you to challenge them. So, if it helps, write your comments in the margins whether you agree or not!

Clarifying or changing organizational values will never be easy. Much inertia is built into systems. Habits run deep and are resistant to change. Sustained effort is needed, especially at in the beginning. An analogy helps to explain the point: a moribund organization is like a motor car that will not start – much effort is needed to get it moving, but once the engine fires it will roar away.

The effort needed to clarify personal and organizational values will be hard to measure. By definition, there are no objective tests to measure the soundness of a value. Acts of faith are required. Debate, reflection, experiment and conscience are essential. But the final result, the organization's value system, should be a subtle consensus which binds everyone together.

Fundamental change cannot be energized from the edge of an organization. Values are decided in the head and heart – top management must be deeply involved. That is why this book is addressed to managers. However, those outside the management group should not feel impotent; within their own area of authority their values really matter.

This book aims to provide a balanced and progressive management philosophy which is realistic, fair, inspiring and positive. This will be the end result of implementing each of the twelve values *at the same time*. There are checks and balances built into the theory which prevent tyranny or exploitation.

We hope you enjoy the process of value clarification, but don't forget, you have to do the work!

Reference

1 Dave Francis, *Unblocking Organizational Communication*, Gower, Aldershot, 1987.

Part II

MANAGING MANAGEMENT

3 Power: Managers must manage

The management group should have the knowledge, authority and organization to decide the mission of the enterprise, acquire resources and make decisions. Successful managers understand the inherent power of their position and take charge of the organization's destiny. They adopt the value: *managers must manage*.

Management holds a unique position in any organization – on top. Only management is in a position to take charge and it must do so. Management should strive to gain and retain effective power.

There have been many cases where management has lost effective power and suffered the dire consequences. At a national level the fortunes of the Lebanon are a chilling reminder of the chaos and inhumanity which follows a breakdown of authority.

We live in an era when the acceptance of authority is under threat. Educational, political and cultural factors have eroded once traditional values, especially over the last thirty years. Hospital nurses used to be treated with respect. Today they are frequently violently assaulted in the casualty wards of inner city hospitals. Petty theft is a way of life for many.

Organizations cannot cut themselves off from the wider society. Managers must cope with a deep reluctance in many people to accept discipline. Successful managements have recognized the anti-authority trends in society and attempted to minimize their corrosive effects.

Sources of power

Power is gained from four sources. Each is dependent on the others. The thesis of this book is that managements should strive to capture all of the sources of power and retain them.

The first source of power is *ownership*. Those who have the legal title to an enterprise have rights. Managers are professional instruments, charged to act in the best interests of the owners. Legitimate authority flows down the management chain of command. This is relatively easy to see in the private sector but in the public sector, especially social services, the organization must be responsible to all of us. Sometimes public bodies create a representative group who, in effect, act as the owners; legitimate authority then flows from this source. Successful managements strengthen the owners, so that they are a potent force – and win them over, so that managers enjoy full support.

The second source of power is *information*. That which is measurable can be managed. The quality of management information systems determines how well those at the top can control and co-ordinate the organization. There have been many cases where effective power could not be exercised because of ignorance of those in command. Successful managements identify the key success factors which affect their industry and ensure that the management information system speedily measures the important things.

The third source of power is *attractiveness*. Managements should be able to win the hearts and minds of employees. Attraction power comes from having a vision of the future based on sound values; then communicating this vision so that people want to be part of making it real. This is the true role of the leader. Successful managements attract people by what they say and what they do.

The fourth source of power is *reward and punishment*. People, unless they are perverse, do what rewards them and avoid that which hurts them. Managers can control the reward/punishment system (as we discuss in greater length in Chapter 5). Crude carrot-and-stick methods are not capable of producing sustained motivation. Successful managements use rewards with subtlety.

Acquiring and retaining these four power sources are the preconditions for gaining effective authority. Maintaining authority is another matter. This requires attention, respect and initiative.

Maintaining authority

You may feel that 'attention' is a strange word to include in a discussion of power. We will explain with an example. The top management group of a German company making ladies' foundation garments in the 1950s was expert at constructing those massive brassieres that characterized the era. Then there was a mood of female rebellion symbolized by the 'burn the bra' movement. The top management group ignored the trend and continued to construct the old-style bras. They went bankrupt and are now remembered only when someone turns up an old undergarment in an attic trunk.

The top managers of our brassiere company lost attention, failed to adapt the corporate mission to the new conditions, and lost their effective power. Henry Mintzberg, in an article on strategy,[1] points out that a successful manager must have an intimate knowledge of the materials with which he or she is working – like the good craftsman. Management must pay attention to detail and maintain the capacity to recognize important changes as they occur. The maintenance of power requires management to make sound decisions at the right time.

Respect is a word much used but difficult to define. It is used when people give others the right to exert influence over them.

The important factor, for managers, is that respect has to be earned. This is done by competence – as we discuss in the next chapter – and clarity about role. The second point requires explanation. Managers, especially those at the top, are responsible for creating the unifying identity of the organization. Only management can answer the fundamental questions 'Where do we want to go?' and 'How do we get there?' A management-defined strategic vision is necessary for organizational health, which means that management must:

- establish the *raison d'être* of the organization
- define the corporate mission
- determine the key success factors of the industry
- establish criteria and means of performance measurement
- build for the future
- care about those whose livelihood and wellbeing depends on its decisions.

If it fails to do that the organization will drift like a ship without a rudder and those who are dependent on the wisdom of managers will quite properly, lose respect and management power will be eroded.

Initiative is closely related to attention, but is active. Management is concerned with getting things done. Power comes from taking timely action. The directors of the brassiere company lost power because they were too slow. We know of one organization which suffered the opposite fate. A local government agency acquired a new director who took hundreds of initiatives – starting studies, introducing techniques, acquiring resources etc. – within his first six months. Much activity was started but the system became over stressed and morale plummeted. The director lost personal power and was replaced. His fault was poor timing. We shall discuss initiative in more depth in Chapters 6-8. For the moment it is sufficient to note that management power depends on action and risk taking.

Sustaining organizational power requires constant vigilance. The following guidelines, derived from careful observation, are helpful to managements who want to sustain power:
* grant high status only to those who have repeatedly demonstrated merit
* when performance slips for a sustained period ensure that the person does not continue to enjoy the fruits of high status
* make sure that those who have high status do not have an easy life
* avoid status symbols which block upwards communication[2]
* do the job that you are paid to do
* ensure that those who report to you do the jobs that they are paid to do.

Dominance

Power is easily confused with dominance, and domination is a dangerous weapon. The desire to have others submit goes deep and the emotions may have a biological or chemical base. Professor Michael McGuire from UCLA studied this issue in his research on the brain chemistry of monkeys on the island of St Kitts. Each colony of monkeys is led by a dominant male who threatens the other males and has the pick of the females. McGuire found that the brain of the dominant male has double the average level of the chemical serotonin in the bloodstream. A dominant male isolated from the submissive gestures of his followers would lose the excess serotonin, but the new lead monkey would double his serotonin within fourteen days. Females do not experience the same chemical reaction. The alarming inference from this research is that the same reaction may occur in executives. In humans, the chemical serotonin is associated with certain kinds of mental disorder – perhaps this is the reason why 'all power corrupts'.

The remedy to the corrupting influence of power is to adhere to the rule (a value drawn from the Christian religion) 'do to others as you would have them do to you'. This forces leaders to display the same attitudes as they seek to encourage.

Managers should understand, acquire and maintain power despite the inherent dangers of an authoritarian approach. We realize that by locating strategic power at the top those lower down the organization have some limits on their freedom. Despite the risks there is no practical alternative; managers must manage.

Authority with responsibility

It has long been a principle of military organization that authority and responsibility should go hand in hand. In practice this is difficult to maintain. Top managers often want to extend their authority down to the level of detail. Despite the difficulties we have found that successful managements place a great deal of emphasis on establishing accountabilities. They adopt the principle that someone should 'have the tools to do the job and be expected to perform'. Responsibility means 'liable to be called to account both practically and ethically'. Exercising authority without responsibility is a licence for abuse; the opposite – responsibility without authority – is unfair and unworkable.

Managements have been forced to move away from the crude authoritarian styles of the past but are learning to cope with the issue of maintaining authority with the support of the workforce. Certainly things are not as bad as they were. One of the authors recalls talking to a night shift supervisor in a food factory in 1974. The man was at his wits' end. His staff simply would not work; they stayed in the cafeteria instead of performing their duties. Physical violence was threatened. Senior management refused to back the supervisor's authority. The result was gross inefficiency and a depressed supervisor who did not know which way to turn. This situation would be much less likely to occur today. Managements have reasserted their right to manage, thereby benefiting themselves, their customers and the communities they serve.

Summary

Core beliefs

- managers must exert discipline
- the 'owners' of the organization should be won over
- a comprehensive management information system is essential
- managements must develop their 'attraction power'
- the reward/punishment system must be controlled
- managers must pay full attention to their task
- respect has to be earned
- timely initiatives must be taken
- managers must discharge their proper role
- high status must be earned
- dominance, for its own sake, should be avoided
- responsibility should go hand in hand with authority.

Five steps to increase the power of management

1 Set up a study group or ask the personnel department to review the limits of authority at each level within your organization. Write the key points on a huge sheet of paper so that all gaps or overlaps can be seen. Clarify all accountabilities and check that the commensurate authorities exist. Are you satisfied the power structure in your organization is sound? Invite all your staff to comment on any changes and redefine roles where necessary.

2 Ask a random sample of people in your organization (department or larger) these two questions: What do you believe are the goals of senior management? and What do you respect about senior management's plans for the future? Record the comments, assess the common themes, and brainstorm practical ways to attract people in your organization to see things your way.[3]

3 Conduct a campaign to increase the support that you receive from above. Find out what your bosses think of you (through informal conversations, reading documents, interviews, written reports etc.) and come to an impartial assessment. Go to great lengths to put across a good impression, concentrating on overcoming any weaknesses. Use professional help to develop effective presentations.

4 Ask all the managers and supervisors in your organization (department or larger) to write an answer to this question: What defects in

the management information system have caused your authority to be weakened over the last three months? Collect the results and invite several experts on management information systems to discuss the problems with you. Managers in large companies will have staff advisers for the purpose.

5 Obtain at least five copies of 'Power Perception Profile (other)' – a validated questionnaire[4] – and the necessary explanatory material. Ask your immediate subordinates to complete a Lead Other form about you. Reflect on the results, and evaluate your personal power profile. Obtain counselling to assist you understand the results, perhaps from your personnel specialist.

References

1 Henry Mintzberg, *Harvard Business Review*, Summer 1987.
2 For further discussion of this point see Dave Francis, *Unblocking Organizational Communication*, Gower, Aldershot, 1987.
3 This project can be formalized using techniques explained in Mike Woodcock and Dave Francis, *Unblocking Your Organization*, Gower, Aldershot, 1990.
4 Available from University Associates International, 45 Victoria Street, Mansfield, Nottinghamshire (tel. 0623 640203).

4 Elitism: Cream at the top

The management task is complex and important. The quality of people who fill management roles is crucial. An inadequate manager can wreak havoc – both sins of commission and of omission. Successful managers understand the vital importance of getting the best possible candidates into management jobs, and continuously developing their competence. They adopt the value: *cream at the top*.

'Those who enjoy power over others need to be an elite. They ought to be selected from those who are superior in intellect and character. They must be carefully trained to discharge their responsibilities with vigour and a sense of duty'. This comment could have been made by a Roman general, a nineteenth-century industrialist or a church leader. In fact, it was made to us by the chairman of a multinational company early in 1988.

The concept of elitism

The *Oxford English Dictionary* defines an elite as 'a group regarded as superior and favoured'. In recent years the concept of elitism has been attacked as divisive and undemocratic. Why do we advocate elitism so strongly?

Some people are inherently more talented than others. The attitudes, skills, knowledge and motivation required to achieve high competence in a specialized field is always limited. This fact should be consciously recognized by management who must do everything in its power to ensure that the most crucial roles in the organization are filled by a 'superior' group.

In most organizations the key role is managerial. This is not always the case. In medical groups, for example, the competence of a surgeon is more vital than the ability of an administrator. However, in non-professional organizations, the decisive resource should always be management. In Chapter 3 we argued that managers must gain and retain power. The responsible use of power is exceptionally demanding. It should not be done by those with average ability. Therefore success-ful managements accept the inevitability of elitism and seek to mitigate its worst features by selecting, controlling and developing elites based on genuine merit.

We have already made a comparison between the task of manage-ment and the craft system of the middle ages. A 'craft' is 'a calling requiring special skill and knowledge' (*Shorter Oxford Dictionary*). Medieval guilds were responsible for supervising the standards of craftsmen. They saw that the development of true competence required seven distinct elements to be mastered before the individual became a member of an elite – a craftsman.

The seven elements are:

- practical skills which allow difficult tasks to be tackled
- intellectual skills to solve problems
- willingness to build for posterity
- explicit ethical standards
- a sense of community with others engaged on the same craft
- a deep understanding of the history and development of their chosen craft
- an awareness of the contribution that their craft makes to the wider community.

The costs of poor managerial craftsmanship are penal. Two examples from our own experience make the point. A rapidly growing food company almost lost control of its cash flow. The company's manage-ment suddenly realized that it was in crisis, despite excellent products and an unrivalled distribution system. Millions were lost but, even worse, top management did not know where the haemorrhages of cash were occurring. Only after an embarrassing investigation could weak-nesses in financial control be pinpointed. The episode, quite properly, was seen by the owners as a lack of financial management craftsmanship – the senior managers were fired.

Our second example is an electrical equipment manufacturer who was widely recognized as an efficient producer of household appliances. Its business was declining as new technologies increasingly made its traditional products obsolete. Top management discussed the problem, but did not take the bold step of investing heavily in research and development. Throughout the company managers were told to do what they knew best: efficiently produce traditional lines. After a six-year decline the company finally shut its doors. The blame lay with senior managers who focused only on short-term problems, and so were poor craftsmen. We shall discuss how to train managerial craftsmen later in this chapter. We believe that everyone who has power over others should be a competent 'managerial craftsman'.

Top quality leadership demands a higher set of competencies and is relatively rare. It must be carefully nurtured. An example makes the point. The American army discovered few soldiers have real leadership ability. They researched the reasons why only a handful of captured men escaped in the Korean war. The reason was that the communist POW guards carefully watched new prisoners and segregated any with leadership potential. These leaders were placed in high-security confinement and watched day and night. About one in twenty received this treatment. The remainder were loosely guarded but lacked leaders to mobilize escape plans. This research suggests that leadership ability is confined to about 5 per cent of the population.

Management (which includes leadership skills) is vital in all kinds of organizations. This was illustrated by a British study in the early 1970s. The government-funded Inspectorate of Schools realized that it could not properly define a 'good' school. A comprehensive research programme meticulously examined every aspect of ten highly regarded and successful schools. The final 1977 report came to the conclusion that the main difference between a 'good' and a 'bad' school was the quality of the head teacher. It is, in essence, the person at the top who determines the effectiveness of thc organization.

Adopting an elitist policy costs a great deal of time and effort. As the coaches for Olympic teams or commanders of elite special regiments will testify: being the best means the ruthless pursuit of superior performance. Elitism can never be a cheap option, but it is the management philosophy practised by successful organizations.

In this chapter we define the beliefs and practices which enable a management elite to be developed. The important issues are selection, training and maintenance of standards. The chapter concludes with a discussion of the risks of employing an elitist policy.

Selection of elites

Who should fill the key roles in organizations? Attributes like intelligence, personality, track record, and skills are important. Equally important, but less often discussed, are the values held by candidates.

Managements have real freedom of choice when they are recruiting or selecting. This is one occasion when the establishment holds an upper hand. We advocate a six-step approach.

1   Define excellence – specify what competencies can be related to superior performance.
2   Use objective measures – use every available technique for avoiding subjective evaluation.
3   Study track record – obtain a detailed and factual record of the individual's actual behaviour under pressure.
4   Explore values – through debate, and a review of past behaviour, try to identify the candidates' values towards management.
5   Test actual competence – use extensive tests, under controlled conditions, to evaluate competence.
6   Explore motivation – a 'hungry' candidate is much more likely to perform well.

This book is not concerned with the detailed techniques which have been covered elsewhere.[1] However, we wish to make one point. Most of the techniques advocated for selection are oriented towards the mass-market. This is not good enough. Managers can learn much from coaches of Olympic teams, commanders of crack military units and leaders of world-famous artistic companies. They know the importance of getting the best raw material and go to any lengths to find extraordinary latent talent.

Some organizations have low standards of selection. Some managers may spend days evaluating the potential cost/benefit of a new machine yet employ an equally costly person after a half-hour chat. If this happens at management level it spells double trouble; the management job is likely to be poorly done and subordinates are stunted and frustrated.

Training

Earlier in this chapter we referred to management as a craft. The training of competent managers requires that the 'apprentice' is introduced to the mysteries of the managerial craft. In an earlier work[2] we identified eleven development areas, each of which is a necessary aspect of managerial craftsmanship. There are eleven key development areas.

1 *Self-management competence.* Management is a demanding task, often sapping mental and emotional energy. The craftsman manager has a deep understanding of time management and keeps fit in every sense of the word.
2 *Clear values.* Managers have to take decisions on what is more or less worthwhile. Such choices should be based on defensible values. The craftsman manager has clear, consistent, tested values which are felt to be right.
3 *Clear goals.* Management is about getting things done despite difficulties, which requires the capacity to focus resources on defined end results. The craftsman manager sets realistic, measurable and challenging goals.
4 *Continuous personal development.* The pace of development is so rapid that managers rapidly become obsolete if their competence does not continue to evolve. People must take responsibility for managing their own development. The craftsman manager deliberately takes steps to grow as a person, and as a manager, throughout life.
5 *Problem-solving skills.* Things going wrong are the daily grind of management. Solutions to non-routine, complex or ambiguous issues must be found. The craftsman manager is a skilful and methodical problem solver.
6 *High creativity.* Machines increasingly perform routine tasks and managers have to deal with novel challenges. This requires both personal creativity and the ability to channel the talents of others. The craftsman manager is able to rise above convention thereby finding new opportunities and solutions to intractable problems.
7 *High influence.* The capacity to persuade others is essential. Scarce resources must be acquired, and influential people won over. Skills such as effective assertion, capable negotiating and persuasive argument are relevant. The craftsman manager is an effective persuader of others – upwards, sideways and below.

8 *Management insight.* Creating the right climate for people to give their best requires management insight. This includes selecting appropriate management styles and motivating others. The craftsman manager creates an open and positive climate which gives people the support and direction that they need.

9 *High supervisory skills.* Much management time is spent juggling resources and reallocating priorities. Organizations must be built, systems constructed and controls established. The craftsman manager is a master of organizational design.

10 *Trainer capacity.* The success of a manager is measured by the efficiency of the unit which he or she controls, which means that continuous development of subordinate skills is needed. This may be done by appraisal, giving feedback, coaching, counselling or direct training. The craftsman manager develops the potential of others.

11 *Team building competence.* People like to feel that they are working with others. Teamwork is important for motivational and practical reasons. Often complex activities are best co-ordinated through informal communication. The craftsman manager is an efficient teambuilder.

Training an elite management group requires attention to each of these eleven areas. Craft competence is primarily developed in the real world. Managers can be helped by education, training and coaching but they must be put in situations where they are required to achieve important results against significant difficulties in the untidy world of daily reality – where pressures, illogicalities and resource shortages are ever present.

The following principles of elite training have proved their worth:

* make the training experience as real as possible
* ensure that the person reflects on their own performance
* give support from proven achievers
* devise training that develops the capacity to endure
* deal with all of the eleven areas identified above.

We are committed to developing outstanding competence in the managerial elite. It is a matter of shame that many managers are less well trained than plumbers. Someone who fixes blocked drains or seized-up ballcock valves will have been taught the plumber's trade. Few managers have received more than rudimentary training and, even worse, they do not take responsibility for their own development.

Maintenance

Any military commander will tell you that even the best troops lose their keenness if they are not constantly being stretched. New challenges must be found and improved techniques of development tried. Managers must form themselves into networks whereby they meet informally to discuss common concerns. It is no surprise that networks are very active in Japan and are regarded by many as the secret of business success. Networks were highly regarded by master craftsmen in the medieval guilds who found that their ideas were updated by debate and shared experience.

Managements can learn from the informal operating practice of the United Kingdom parliament. Members of Parliament spend much of their time together in the Palace of Westminster; in tea rooms, smoking rooms, lounges and bars, there are almost unique networking opportunities. Much of the wisdom that has emanated from Parliament over the centuries has been a direct result of the networking opportunities. In particular, the level of confrontation is sharp and merciless, which eliminates the natural tendency to complacency in established organizations.

The risks of elitism

Remember the dictionary definition of an elite – a superior and *favoured* group. Whenever a group gains privileges there are risks that the power will be ill-used and the unfavoured groups will resent their subordinate position. Some interesting research by Wendy Hirsh[3] shows that a 'blue-eyed boys' syndrome often develops where potential rather than performance is used for selection. These people receive undue attention and an unfair proportion of resources. The management group becomes a self-perpetuating cadre of image-mongers rather than an elite of proven achievers. Hirsh describes the high flyer as 'the right kind of chap. They flash around looking clever, young, quick and keen, saying all the trendy things.' Such people are dangerous. Members of elites, like the master craftsmen of yesterday, must have demonstrated their capability through performance in the real world.

Yet elites must be favoured. Unusual talent and dedication is rare and will go unnoticed unless it is recognized. As we will see in the next chapter, management must be well rewarded in order to sustain an elite resource.

Summary

Core principles

- management should be an elite
- some people are naturally more talented than others
- elites should be chosen only on the criterion of merit
- it is helpful to define management as a craft
- the quality of the elite determines the success of the organization
- adopting an elitist policy is a major managerial commitment
- greatest possible care should be taken when recruiting and selecting managers
- comprehensive training (in the eleven areas described above) is essential
- training techniques should be really stretching
- the 'blue eyed boys' syndrome should be avoided
- elites must be favoured, but this should be done with caution.

Five steps to bring the cream to the top of the milk

1   Encourage the concept of self-development for managers. *The Unblocked Manager*[2] describes a technique for doing this. Obtain a copy of the book, undertake the diagnostic sections, and work through the programme. If it is helpful, take your subordinates through the same process, setting up discussion groups to act as a self-development network.

2   Ask those involved in the selection of managers to spend several days shadowing the best managers in your department. This will give them experience of the real needs. Ask the personnel specialists to develop selection techniques which are based on performance and discuss their ideas in great depth.

3   Invite coaches or captains of winning sports teams to visit your organization and describe how they select and train their athletes. Arrange an informal seminar with your colleagues. Discuss how you can emulate the successful practices of the sports teams in your own organization.

4   Use teambuilding at the top of your organization to develop an elite. The methods and questionnaires in *Team Development Manual*[4] and *Improving Work Groups*[5] help this to be done.

5   Invite everyone responsible for management training in your orga-

nization to write a 1000 word paper entitled 'Good management is
. . .'. Ask your team to evaluate the results against its own views
and principles. Enter into a detailed debate with trainers so that they
are fully aware of your needs and wants.

References

1   See John Jones and Mike Woodcock, *Manual of Management Development*, Gower, Aldershot, 1986.
2   Mike Woodcock and Dave Francis, *The Unblocked Manager*, Gower, Aldershot, 1982.
3   *Institute of Manpower Studies Review*, University of Sussex, June 1985.
4   Mike Woodcock, *Team Development Manual*, second edition, Gower, Aldershot, 1989.
5   Dave Francis and Don Young, *Improving Work Groups*, University Associates, San Diego, 1979.

5 Reward: Performance is king

The performance of those who lead organizations is crucial. Managers must perform consistently and energetically in pursuit of the organization's goals. Successful managers identify and reward success. They adopt the value: *performance is king*.

As consultants on organizational effectiveness we are often asked to help companies that have lost their way and are struggling to survive. It is a difficult task. Invariably there are a host of problems: poor systems, untrained staff, inadequate investment, low morale, weak marketing, high costs and so on.

One such organization we shall call The Metal Skills Company. It occupied a rundown site in the back streets of a traditional manufacturing town. For years the company had been on the brink of bankruptcy. We were asked by Bob Greenway, the chief executive, to advise on improvements and we undertook a thorough study. As usual, almost every organizational ailment known to man was present. The sickness was apparent to all; only the solution remained obscure.

Fortunately, The Metal Skills Company made a range of products that were marketable. The main problem was that the manufacturing procedures were wasteful, ponderous, costly, uncontrolled and overmanned. We advised that all management efforts be directed towards a radical overhaul of the manufacturing system. This meant introducing 'just in time' manufacture for low-cost flexibility, 'total product quality' for improved standards and 'quality circles' for increased employee involvement.

Such changes required a revolution in attitudes, skills, behaviour and organization. Bob Greenway became convinced of the need for change intellectually, but not emotionally. We suggested that he should visit a number of factories in Japan and Korea. He returned white-faced, daunted but resolute. From then onwards the change programme received his wholehearted support: he had seen the strength of the enemy. He addressed a staff meeting saying: 'We have no option. We must compete or die. I am to blame for waking up too slowly to the challenge that we face. But I have learnt my lesson. From today, every action that we take must be questioned. We must review all our habits, and discard those which do not add value to our products. One principle must underlie everything that we do – it is results that count. Everything else is irrelevant. There are no legitimate excuses.'

The effects of Bob Greenway's speech were disappointing. Some employees felt that the speech was a scaremongering trick, whilst others were confused by the new concepts. Nothing changed. Bob Greenway decided on a bold investment; he sent a group of ten managers, supervisors and trade union representatives to retrace his steps around the manufacturing plants of Japan and Korea. He chose the group carefully, selecting those whose opinions guided others.

The effect was electric. The group returned belligerent in their desire to transform The Metal Skills Company into a 'world class manufacturing unit'. Another important investment was made. A six-hour set of videos on new manufacturing philosophies was purchased. Everyone, from sweeper to general manager, in the manufacturing division saw these videos twice. They learned that Japanese managers in the Toyota company had perfected 'just in time' techniques in the 1960s and 1970s. Industry in the USA had discovered the benefits in 1980 when General Electric, Kawasaki and Toyota trucks (in Long Beach) began to use the concepts.

The Metal Skills Company's management felt that it had to go down the same route. It had attempted participative management a decade earlier but the benefits had been transient. The problem is well known. As Robert Reich[1] put it: 'Management consultants espoused "Theory Y" or, better still, "Theory Z". But these factory-tested techniques for making workers feel better simply created a facade of workplace collaboration. The distinction between thinkers and doers remained intact'. This time the company management decided to commit itself to a total revolution. Task groups were established to install Just in Time manufacture, Total Product Quality and Quality Circles. Much research was done. No longer was the company ignorant of the techniques needed.

Within two years The Metal Skills Company was exporting to Japan and its renaissance was featured in the national press. It had ruthlessly eliminated wasteful systems and behaviour. It was proud of its international competitiveness. How had it been achieved? The Metal Skills Company had adopted the value: performance is king.

The value 'performance is king' had to become part of the company's culture. This meant that the reward system had to be changed. In this chapter we will examine rewards, which shape the values of the total organization.

Benefits are largely controlled from the top of the organization, and are the manager's tool kit for shaping behaviour at work. Reward and punishment are primary techniques for influencing and controlling others. The ability to reward and punish is a source of power. The saying 'he who pays the piper calls the tune' is true, at least in part. Successful managements use reward and punishment systems for aligning organizations towards sustaining high performance.

It has taken a long time for the creative power of the reward system to be recognized by managers. For example, Rank Xerox was reported in the press in 1988[2] when it announced that the merit payments for its senior managers would partly depend on customers' feedback. An annual survey was to be conducted: if customers thought ill of the firm then the poor feedback reduced the pay of the responsible managers. It is surprising that such measures were not in place years earlier.

Reward and punishment affect (condition) the way we behave. People, like other animals, seek satisfaction whilst avoiding pain. How should people be rewarded so that they will adopt the value 'performance is king'?

Reward power can be used in five key ways; consider these illustrations:

1 *Attracting able people.* We need a brilliant chemist. Search the world. Make an offer that can't be refused.
2 *Demonstrating relative value.* Top-quality sales personnel are vital. We will pay them as much as the chief executive.
3 *Showing that merit wins the day.* Jones has succeeded where Smith did not. We will promote Jones.

4   *Shaping behaviour*. From 1 January sales personnel will have an increased proportion of their earnings related to the degree of satisfaction of their customers.

5   *Integrating effort*. Every department is expected to present its plans for improving interdepartmental communication within one month.

Reward systems actually influence the thinking process. This was well described by one manager who said: 'In our company managers are paid a 10 per cent bonus on profitability against targets. If we don't meet target – then we don't get the bonus: it's as simple as that. We also get a 1 per cent additional bonus for each percentage point of profit over 10 per cent – up to a maximum of bonus 20 per cent in total.

This year began well and senior managers relaxed, spending a lot of time long-term planning. Then our margins came under threat and it's now hell for leather to make budget. No-one talks about the bonus but, like the threat of imminent hanging, it certainly concentrates the mind.'

Reward systems should be devised to reinforce high performance. The example in the preceding paragraph illustrates the point. Current theories of motivation provide useful guidelines. 'Expectancy theory' is now widely accepted and the lessons are of real practical value. The key points are:

- attitudes, beliefs, values and perceptions should be studied in great detail; well constructed attitude surveys are a useful tool with which to gain this information
- rewards are best related to individual performance, not given as general rises
- people should know exactly how rewards are allocated so that it is quite obvious that high performance brings high reward; this requires an effective communication programme
- training should emphasize that high rewards can be realized through high performance
- everyone's goals should be clearly identified and managers should strive to remove blockages to goal attainment
- those who support non-productive values should be encouraged to realize that these do not lead to success in the long term.

Adopting these six guidelines is a practical way of saying that 'performance is king'. The first battle is to win the hearts and minds of the management cadre. In turn, managers shape the attitudes and values of all employees. Senior managers should use the reward system to align thinking, by creating a definition of organizational 'reality' which moulds people's values and standards into a consistent pattern, acting like a magnet on iron filings.

Rewards are sometimes given for no objective performance achievement. People's behaviour goes haywire and management lacks the tools to re-establish standards. An analogy comes from the People's Republic of China, where the government conducted a study on the problem of the notoriously rude shop assistants of Peking. The 1984 report found that it was commonplace to see customers pleading with idle shop workers for service, even weeping to get a response. Rudeness, incivility and even physical violence were observed. The government report explained that shop staff had total security of employment, with their bonuses and wages guaranteed, and so lacked any incentive to perform to an acceptable level. Since the report was published action was taken. Shop staff are now increasingly being measured by performance, like other parts of the Chinese economy. On a recent visit Mike Woodcock observed the great effects these changes are having on the general well being: 'It is, in part, the reward system adopted by the Chinese Government that is bringing about radical change and new found prosperity'.

The 'performance is king' value has two implications. The first is that everyone must have an accurate personal definition of excellent performance and the second is that non-performance related activities must be pruned back.

The technique of Management by Objectives emphasizes that everyone should know what outputs are required from their work but be allowed to choose the means of accomplishment. This is the essential ingredient in performance management. The MBO ritual – an annual cycle, full documentation and formalized procedures – is often unhelpful, but the intention is right. As users of the techniques in the best selling *One Minute Manager*[3] will realize, the basic tenets of Management by Objectives are invaluable.

Much organizational resource is often wasted on tangential activities. This tendency has to be watched. Energy diverted to things which are 'nice' rather than essential can erode the obsessive commitment characteristic of successful organizations. Performance, for its own sake, is the driving force. The successful manager inculcates a principle that results are the first criterion of success with the dedication of a mountain climber who risks his life to reach the top of a difficult peak: because it is there.

Despite all their good intentions managers often find it difficult to implement the 'performance is king' principle. How do you measure the contribution of the public relations manager, or the head teacher in a school? It is difficult, but not impossible, to quantify. In such cases worth can only be assessed by comparing the person's performance against a standard. In our consulting practice we have found these six reward strategies to be a useful practical guide:

1   Be explicit about what constitutes success in each job.
2   Reward 'positive' behaviour with above average material benefits.
3   Reward 'positive' behaviour with above average recognition.
4   Use all possible persuasion techniques (leadership, media, communication etc.) to relate group norms to high performance.
5   Create opportunities for people to feel good about using their skills and knowledge.
6   Deal with low standards of performance.

There are many difficulties in implementing these six reward strategies. It is easier in the management group because they are disposed to be supportive. Successful organizations find ways of taking the 'performance is king' ethic down to the lowest level.

However, there is a common barrier which applies to some management groups and many other parts of the workforce. Both managers and trade unionists realized long ago that reward and punishment systems are crucial devices for achieving compliance. Historically, trade unions have sought to reduce managerial power by standardizing payment structures on a non-performance basis. Since a 'good' employee performs much better than a 'bad' employee it must be a principle of successful managements that they, not trade unions, control the policies of the organizational reward/punishment system.

All the managers that we have asked believe in inequality. They are troubled because it is difficult to recognize and reward the real differences between people. For example, many craftsmen who have given thirty years of excellent service have inferior status and privileges to their seventeen-year-old typist daughters who are classed as white-collar staff. The principle is clear: managers must recognize and reward high performance.

Reward/punishment systems meet this requirement if they are:

• based on a fair and equitable method of measuring performance
• easy to understand

- straightforward to monitor
- flexible to meet unpredicted needs
- supported by the representatives of relevant interest groups
- linked to career and performance improvement.

Financial reward is an imperfect motivator. It has been wisely said, 'the promise of a good salary will get someone to work each day but it won't encourage hard work'. The psychological rewards – challenge, recognition, fear of failure and personal power – must be employed. Above all there is one basic motivator – belonging. People are, at root, tribal animals. The sophistication of the human race is relatively recent. Insightful managers take advantage of people's basic need to belong by making them feel valued only when they are performing to a high standard. Managers have to realize that they are the emotional leaders of their departments and organizations.

Low levels of performance can usually be observed when psychological rewards are neglected. Successful managements use rewards to energize people and get them working for the organization. They train all their managers to implement the subtle motivational techniques which give challenge, provide recognition, set demanding targets and enable people to feel genuinely important contributors.

We conclude this chapter with some cautionary words. The relentless drive for performance can become, using the words of Roger Harrison, an experienced analyst of management cultures, 'demonic'.[4] By this he means that moral standards are discarded in a ruthless search for output and profit. Performance should be king, but not God.

Summary

Core principles

- reward and punishment are primary techniques for influencing and controlling others
- rewards should be used to align people to work for management's goals
- managerial rewards must be related to performance
- the expectancy theory of motivation should be carefully studied by managers

- everyone should understand the reward system
- people should focus their attention on results, not diversions
- positive behaviour should always be rewarded
- negative behaviour cannot be allowed to go unchallenged
- every system or convention which undermines fair reward for performance must be fought
- managers must be expert in non-financial rewards
- a performance culture must not be allowed to become 'demonic'.

Five steps for rewarding performance

1   Invite a management psychologist from a business school to arrange a half-day seminar for your team on 'Reward and punishment in management'. Tell the psychologist that you want to hear a summary of the latest research, including the work of Professor Lawler.[5] Discuss the effectiveness of your current approach to rewarding high performance and confronting low performance. Conclude with a checklist of action steps.

2   Explore ways of training your managers to be more skilful in giving psychological rewards. Techniques such as job enrichment,[6] giving positive feedback,[7] transactional analysis[8] and coaching[9] are useful. Ask your training department to prepare a course. Ensure that plenty of skill practice is built in. Attend the pilot course, in full, before you commit your managers to attending.

3   Study the policies on rewards of any staff associations or trade unions. Get to know the officials of these organizations to see how they think. See whether there are any means of strengthening the payment for performance principle in practice.

4   Recognize the need to change your incentive system every few years. There is much evidence that such systems lose their effectiveness over time. Adopt a policy of continuous experimentation to see what new techniques for increasing incentive might be of value.

5   Collect data from the managers, and any other relevant groups, about what motivates and demotivates them. Use a validated questionnaire for the purpose.[10] Your personnel manager, or a competent consultant, will be able to help. Arrange for the results of the survey to be presented to a meeting of your team and decide on practical steps to improve motivation. Set targets and regularly monitor the effectiveness of your programme.

References

1 Robert Reich, *The New American Frontier*, Times Books, New York, 1983, p. 75.
2 *Financial Times*, London, 17 February 1988.
3 Kenneth Blanchard and Spencer Johnson, *The One Minute Manager*, Collins, London, 1988.
4 Roger Harrison, 'Strategies for a New Age' in *Human Resource Management*, vol. 22, no. 3, Autumn 1983, pp. 209–35.
5 Edward E. Lawler, *Pay and Organizational Effectiveness: a Psychological View*, McGraw-Hill, 1971.
6 Frederick Herzberg, *Work and the Nature of Man*, Staples Press, New York, 1968.
7 See Blanchard and Johnson above.
8 Eric Berne, *Games People Play*, Penguin Books, Harmondsworth, 1968.
9 Hawdon Hague, *Management Development for Real*, Institute of Personnel Management, London 1973.
10 A suitable questionnaire can be obtained from Teleometrics, Chartwell-Bratt (Publishing and Training), Old Orchard, Bickley, Bromley, Kent BR1 2NE.

Part III

MANAGING THE TASK

6 Effectiveness: Doing the right thing

Focusing on the right issues must be a constant preoccupation. Unless effort is well directed, somewhere a smarter management will find ways of taking your market. Successful managers are able to focus resources on activities which get results. They adopt the value: *do the right thing.*

In the back streets of a prosperous city a scientific instrument manufacturer locked its doors for the last time. Founded in the 1920s by an entrepreneurial scientist who had pioneered a new technique for analyzing trace chemical elements, the company became a watchword for manufacturing reliable and innovative products. For many years it had been world famous and, about ten years ago, the prosperous company was purchased from its elderly owner by a multinational conglomerate on a buying spree. New management was installed under a 'professional' chief executive – a distinguished accountant a few years from retirement.

Under the new chief executive's stewardship things did not go well. Investment was pruned with savage contempt for anything but immediate advantage, new products were not developed and corporate vitality evaporated. Competitors saw the weakness in their most respected rival and seized the market. Orders slowed to a trickle. The chief executive cut investment even further as he strove to balance the books. Older employees witnessed the destruction of their once proud company and boldly stated that the new management policy was wrong. They were ignored. Those with marketable skills left for new jobs whilst

51

the longest serving employees soldiered on with grim foreboding.

One bright summer's day two chauffeur-driven limousines visited the factory. The men from corporate head office had arrived. They spent half the day touring the plant, inspecting the doleful accounts and concluded by deciding to close the company.

The story has a sad ending. Craftsmen, instrument makers, assemblers and clerical workers had spent their lives contributing their excellent skills, but were thrown out of work with nothing more than a standardized word-processed letter of regret from a distant executive.

What was the cause of the decline and fall of the scientific instrument company? Simple. The new chief executive did the wrong thing – time and time again.

There are many reasons for decline. Stuart Slatter[1] has made a study of those companies which have gone into near-terminal decline and he concludes that the most powerful poison is a domineering chief executive who fails to listen.

The other reasons why commercial companies fail make salutary reading. They are:

- an ineffective top team – either weak individuals, functionally specific contributions, poor communication and/or a lack of consensus
- neglect of the core business – frittering away energy on divergent issues
- lack of management depth – having inexperienced, under-educated or low-achieving individuals in key positions
- complacent belief in evolution – not seeing the need for radical change.

All these factors can create a situation in which managers do the wrong thing. We argued in Chapter 3 that power must be grasped by management, that the key decisions should always be taken by the senior management group. There can be no valid excuses if the organization is misdirected. Only the management can be blamed for indecision or wrong decision.

No-one can guarantee right decision making at the top. In the end a decision is a combination of analysis, hunch, hope and belief. Decision making is a fallible process, limited by the knowledge and talent of those with power. However, all is not lost. Much can, and should be done to improve the knowledge of decision makers, enhance the talents of the top team and improve the process by which all the necessary ingredients come together.

As we emphasized in Chapter 4, it is vital to ensure that the apex of the organization is staffed with able people. It is one of the ironies of management life that, despite millions of unemployed, talented and available senior executives are as rare as banknotes lying in the street. Even when able individuals are recruited the story has only just begun.

Pioneering work by Meredith Belbin[2] (discussed further in Chapter 10) demonstrated that senior management teams who are capable of doing things right are built with diverse individuals. His analysis shows, we think conclusively, that the basis of wise decision making is a balanced top team.

However, simply assembling the right ingredients does not make a good cake! The members of a top team must understand that their role is quite distinct from middle management. They are the guardians of mission and strategy. Fundamental decisions about values, resources, priorities, tactics and aims can only be taken at the top. The senior management group must have a shared understanding of the 'legacy' that they wish to leave behind them. (This is especially true for non-commercial organizations.) Such strategic decision making requires specialized expertise – just as a steeplejack requires different skills from a bricklayer.

Suppose that the organization has an able, balanced and skilled top team – is this all that is required? The answer is 'no'! An effective management process has to be in place. Managers can learn much about effective decision-making processes from studying the ways that the world's most important issues are resolved in government. In the example that we know best, the British parliamentary model, there are a number of conventions that serve to improve the quality of decision making.

1   Key issues are exhaustively debated by people with varied points of view.
2   No-one allows politeness to prevent vigorous probing and questioning.
3   Opposition is deliberately encouraged.
4   People with special interests are invited to put their point of view.
5   There is a huge machine designed to provide valid information for the decision makers.
6   Those who take decisions are forcefully reminded of the outcomes

of their choices later.
7 Lying is seen as unacceptable.

The important insights gained from studying the parliamentary model are that decision making should never be allowed to happen in a 'closed system'. Those at the top should be constantly challenged, made to be truthful and held accountable. When this happens there is a much greater possibility that the right things will be done. Doing the right thing is more likely when open government prevails. By exposing issues honestly, using the guidelines that parliament has evolved over the centuries, the chances of wise decision making are increased.

For commercial companies this means having a strategy for sustaining a competitive edge. From Michael Porter[3] we learn that there are only three distinct competitive strategies – being the cheapest (cost leadership), being special (differentiation) or spotlighting a narrow area for concentration (focus). It is vitally important that top managers understand which competitive strategy they should use and ruthlessly pursue their chosen direction.

For example, General Motors, in most of the countries in which they operate, seek to be the cost leader. They aggressively seek market share so that they can enjoy economies of scale, vigorously pursue cost reduction, keep a strangle hold on overheads, avoid low volume markets and study the costs of competitors. Another company, Porsche, chooses to differentiate – with the aim of being seen by the customer as providing a significantly better product. It invests in being perceived as unique, finding valued differences and being either fashionable or novel. The strategies of both companies are very different and, in order to do the right thing, everyone in the company needs to know exactly what is important. Mike Woodcock has visited production plants of each and talked to senior management in each. They are both successful. They both do the right thing, but in different ways.

Non-commercial organizations have a more complex task in establishing their mission. One organization may see its purpose as contributing to sustaining current patterns of life (like the police force); another may define its role as helping to build a better future (as a theatre may aim to do). Since there is no standardized way to measure 'contribution to the social good' strategic decision makers in such organizations are well advised to use something like the parliamentary process described above in order to improve the quality of their top management process and find a viable mission.

Many senior managers are well aware of their decision-making responsibilities. The chairman of a large public company told us: 'Above all I must be positive and realistic. Excessive optimism will place the company in jeopady. Pessimism, on the other hand, stunts initiative and stultifies creative minds. Realism is more difficult; if I make wrong judgements then I lead people astray. My task is to do everything possible to see that the right judgements are made at the right time.'

Once the mission is clear the task has only just begun. Doing the right thing requires a commitment to evaluate factual data and confront reality. Managers should be practical scientists who do not fall into the trap of defining subjective perception as truth. They must define systems which collect and organize strategic data. As any army commander will tell you, this is at the heart of effective decision making.

Constructs for organization

Management consultant Bob Garratt[4] says that the subconscious ways in which managers organize their thought processes (psychologists call the patterns 'constructs') are vitally important. The notion makes excellent sense. A manager who sees the organizational world in terms of entries on a balance sheet is unlikely to perceive or respect qualitative data. Garratt describes four basic constructs which senior managers use to guide them. Each has its limitations, and managers who fail to use all four are liable to do the wrong thing, especially those who, in Garratt's words, are 'bound by the conceptual shackles of traditional specializa tion'.

Adapting Garratt's thinking we can define four models.

The functionalist view

Top managers see their world in terms of the classic functions like production, sales, finance etc. They pay some attention to the environment and their markets, but through the existing organizational structure. Typically such organizations have little teamwork at the top; there is little to discuss as most tasks are broken down into functional responsibilities.

The functionally responsive view

Top managers continue to see the world in functional terms but develop their teamwork so that they deal with a wider range of issues, like social and economic changes and issues of ethics. Managers still see themselves as heads of functions, but the quality of debate is much improved.

The power groupings view

Top managers see their task in terms of dealing with those who have power over the organization. This includes the owners, the public, the consumers, and those who provide labour or inputs into the system. When top managers take this viewpoint they are less likely to be trapped into interpreting everything through functional blinkers.

The competitive quality view

Top managers define what their organization does that gives value to the world. They think about four aspects: the quality of business performance, the quality of consumer service, the quality of working life, and the quality of social responsibility. This way of thinking focuses attention on contribution and requires careful identification of the ingredients of competitiveness. It leads to defining the organization's task in terms of worth. So a commercial company that thinks in this way will be concerned with the reasons why customers should be satisfied, and sees profitability as a measure of success.

There is no single right way to think about management. Flexibility in the use of constructs is the key to success. Able managers look at their world in a number of different ways, conducting a series of intellectual experiments and building up a comprehensive picture from many fragmented insights.

The Japanese, who are no strangers to organizational success, adopt a particularly focused approach to improving the quality of decision making. They emphasize the importance of allowing time for thought by using the techniques of meditation and consensus. They realize that some decisions are much more important than others and it pays to invest a great deal of thought to get the basics right.

For the western observer the process seems to move with almost painful slowness. Options are discussed over and over again. Time is allocated to meditate on the issues and see what the intelligence of the unconscious mind says on the issue. Consensus is sought even when the majority share a common view. Finally, when a decision is taken, the process has brought two advantages: depth and commitment. The ground rules ensure that issues are examined in depth and so the chances of superficial analysis are minimal. Secondly, everyone concerned has played a part in the decision and understands the commitments needed. The entire management team moves with speed and clarity – it is like the story of the tortoise and the hare played on a huge scale.

There is one final idea that we must describe. It is wrong to imagine that a well constructed and able team with efficient psychological and operational processes will always succeed. In its competence there lurks a destructive worm. It was a political scientist, Professor Janus,[1] who opened our eyes to a great enemy of right decision making which he called 'groupthink'. When important decisions have to be made often it is natural for a small group of powerful people to determine what should be done. This avoids the convoluted complexity of democratic systems and the obvious risk of tyranny in a despotic regime. However, Janus found that the members of close groups begin to think alike, look only to others within the group for support, and ignore all evidence which suggests that their views are wrong. Such groups unconsciously establish 'mind guards' who prevent disturbing facts from being heard and they feel themselves to be superior in wisdom. Their decision making becomes suspect and travesties of judgement are common place. Ironically, the closeness of the decision-making team contributes to the decline in its capacity as effective decision maker.

These are the managerial ingredients which increase the chances that management will do the right thing. In the end there is no remedy for incompetence in positions of power. But much can be done to reduce risks and confront problems as they occur. For the sake of all those who work in the organization, and are affected by it, it is vital to work continuously to do the right thing.

Summary

Core principles

- domination is dangerous

- management cannot escape its responsibility for decision making
- every care should be taken to ensure that there is an able and balanced top team
- top managers must understand every aspect of their role
- senior managers must have a shared understanding of the legacy that they wish to leave
- an effective management information system is the basis of good decision making
- managers can learn much from reviewing the work of political decision-making systems
- no organization should be a closed system
- commercial organizations must be 100 per cent clear about their competitive strategy
- it pays to look at the management task from a number of different perspectives
- meditation and consensus seeking are valuable tools in the pre-decision phase
- 'groupthink' should be understood and avoided.

Five steps to encourage 'doing the right thing'

1   Develop the decision-making skills of senior managers. Ask several business schools to put together a presentation after looking at your needs. Invite their consultants to attend your senior team meetings to get first hand understanding of your strengths and weaknesses.

2   Identify your three best competitors and collect information about their decision-making mechanisms. Perhaps set up a project group to conduct a detailed comparison between you and the opposition. Plot the key decisions that they have taken on a historical graph showing their performance. Study how they approached the decision-making task and try to learn the lessons.

3   Obtain a copy of The Groupthink Audit[6] and ask senior teams to complete it. This will help assess the strengths and weaknesses of the top team's decision making from a psychological viewpoint. Perhaps an experienced team facilitator would be helpful. The Audit contains practical suggestions about techniques for reducing the risk of groupthink.

4   Experiment with the services of a 'non-executive director' to contribute to decision making at senior levels. Invite an experienced

manager to act as a catalyst in decision-making meetings. Try a number of different individuals, to study the effect of different personalities and skills.

5   Set up a video camera at several senior team meetings and find an editor to produce a half-hour film which typifies the process of the meeting. Show the video immediately prior to the next meeting and ask the group to brainstorm ways of improving the team's process.

References

1   Stuart Slatter, *Corporate Recovery*, Penguin Books, Harmondsworth, 1987.
2   Meredith Belbin, *Management Teams - Why They Succeed and Fail*, Heinemann, 1981.
3   Michael Porter, *Competitive Strategy*, Free Press, New York, 1980.
4   Bob Garratt, *The Learning Organization*, Fontana/Gower, 1987, pp. 66–70.
5   I.L. Janus, *Victims of Groupthink*, Harcourt Brace Jovanovich, London, 1972.
6   In Dave Francis, *50 Activities for Unblocking Organizational Communication*, Gower, Aldershot, 1987.

7 Efficiency: Doing things right

It has been said that good management is about doing hundreds of little things well. All too often a small error makes an out-of-proportion effect on the quality of the whole. The drive to do everything well gives a sharp edge. Successful managers relentlessly search for better ways to do things, and they constantly build pride in the job. They adopt the value: *do things right*.

We began writing this chapter on a flight from London to New Zealand, via Denver. The journey had started badly. Mike had driven a hundred and fifty miles down congested roads. We arrived just in time for the flight.

As we struggled onto the plane the cabin staff watched us with laconic disinterest. Dave was carrying his portable computer, a large bag of papers and a suit bag. But we were looking forward to the luxury of faultless first-class airline service, imagining that our journey would be like a TV advertisement. Needless to say, the opposite was the case. We were shown to our seats by a flight attendant who behaved with the warmth of a prison warder. She used the 'correct' phrases, no doubt taught to her in airline school, but the demeanour was jaded and her concern was plastic. We began to get settled for the twenty-five-hour flight. Dave's bag would not fit into the front wardrobe, and the flight attendant barked 'Take it to the larger closet by the exit'. Then she vanished, leaving him to struggle with an overstuffed garment bag against the human tide. Meanwhile Mike's every request to the cabin staff met with a grudging acquiesence. During the journey we noticed several minor incidents, innuendoes, oversights and slipshod errors of service. We both felt like passengers on a commuter bus journey, not first-class international jetsetters. From one point of view the blemishes were minor, and it would have seemed petty to complain, but our memory of the flight is sour and it is doubtful whether we will willingly fly this airline again. In a hundred ways the flight staff 'did the wrong thing'.

Somewhere over the Atlantic we began to think about our situation from a management point of view. What would we do if we were senior executives of that airline? No doubt they had debated the image they wanted to present and had enshrined their customer service standards in a well-phrased charter. But the reality of that bright October morning was different. The crew went through the motions, but they did not care. We tried to understand the causes of the mediocre service and found ourselves analysing categories of organization where there was a demonstrated concern to do things right.

Our first line of enquiry was historic. Why was it that Great Britain, a small island with few obvious advantages, had become the birthplace of the Industrial Revolution and, for many years, the world's most successful economy?

The answer can be found, in part, in an analysis of social values. From the early eighteenth century a new spirit of invention, entrepreneurship and dedication began to thrive. It became commonplace for machines to do the work of people. Efficient (for the times) factories replaced independent craftsmen. Increasingly wealth was created by industrial enterprise, rather than by agriculture. By the time Queen Victoria came to the throne Britain was the 'workshop of the world'. It is illuminating to examine the factors which led to such a successful combination of attitudes and behaviour. (After all, most managers, including airline executives, are trying to stimulate a similar process in their own organizations today.)

Perhaps the best explanation of the causes of the British Industrial Revolution was, ironically, presented by the German Max Weber, whose book *The Protestant Ethic and the Spirit of Capitalism*[1] presented a profound analysis. The title says it all. Weber argued that protestant beliefs influenced the personalities of people so that they believed that they should fulfil themselves by achievement and hard work in this world, rather than by devoting themselves to contemplating the life hereafter. Eighteenth-century Britain, almost alone in the world, was a society without a fatalistic acceptance of the status quo.

The motto 'If a job is worth doing, it is worth doing well' became current. Hard work was seen as virtuous, and the embryonic middle class epitomized the diligent values of the times.

Many of the inspired founders of the Industrial Revolution shared the ethics of the nineteenth-century American pioneers. They believed that personal values were important and that everyday life had a meaning above mere self-interest. People were taught to believe that one's merit in this life was dependent on the amount of care and attention that was invested in the tasks of each day.

This simple belief gave direction to the greatest changes in economic productive capacity in the history of mankind. The principles advocated were that people are responsible for their fortunes in life, and their fortune depends on diligence and attention to detail. The same theme occurred in all walks of life. Baden Powell's oft repeated advice to the Boy Scout movement that 'stickability' is a primary virtue led to generations of young people striving to see things through.

Times change and the Protestant Ethic is no longer an inspiration in many people's lives, especially the cabin crew on that flight to Denver. If the history books are to be believed many nineteenth-century workers possessed the attitudes that most managers would like to see displayed today. Today's managers face a dilemma; they need people to adopt diligent attitudes, yet cannot rely on the accepted social values to inculcate them.

Behaviour is based on well articulated and frequently repeated beliefs which are held as precious by those who shape opinions in the community. If the values of the wider society do not support efficiency and effectiveness, then managers have no option; they must fight against the current social trends and inculcate the right values. They have to win the battle for the hearts of the workforce.

Successful organizations are capable of doing this. They have learnt the boring but essential truth that 'doing things right' is an essential ethic. The modern form of this evergreen insight is the Quality Improvement Programmes that companies like IBM, Scandinavian Airways and Woolworth have undertaken. A managing director conveyed the principle exactly when he commented to us: 'Persistence is everything. When people set inner standards their performance is improved from within. This means that people take greater responsibility for their working likes. This is the ethos that I try to create. But it's a hard battle. Society has largely lost the standards of hard work. Many people want something for nothing. We have to swim against the tide, but when this is done the individual feels a great satisfaction – pride of accomplishment.'

It is possible to develop an organizational culture that promotes 'doing things right'. In many countries the elite army regiments are masters of the art. But successful concerns as diverse as hamburger stores, opera houses and prisons have shown that it is possible to devise and sustain a high-performing culture.

The recent history of Jaguar cars is a case in point. It will not surprise you to learn that 'doing things right' was an obsession of Sir William Lyons, the founder of the Jaguar company. But his ethic was lost when this once-proud sports car manufacturer was swallowed up by a margantian bureaucracy in a fit of government-inspired 'rationalization'. In the late 1970s Jaguar was virtually bankrupt. It had a fine basic product, a skilful but inefficient workforce, and a potentially viable niche in the market. But the product quality was appalling. When John Egan became managing director in 1980, he displayed a singleminded determination to remedy the lack of care which had plagued every aspect of production. The whole company had to rediscover the merits of doing things right. This began with suppliers, and touched every aspect of production, marketing, sales and customer care. The programme of organizational relearning was achieved through management development, intensive communication, pruning of 'dead wood', worker involvement and the development of efficient control systems. A relentless 'pursuit of perfection' was the only solution to Jaguar's problems.

Organizations have no choice but to work on developing a diligent culture. Competition from countries in the Pacific Basin is razor sharp. A colleague returned from a month's study tour of Japan and remarked: 'They don't have any secrets, they just follow through on everything. Western companies must rediscover the spirit of quality'.

How is this to be done? Senior managers must be fully committed to the principle of doing things right. Then the message must be cascaded down throughout the organization. The processes needed are persuasion and indoctrination. Both words smack of brainwashing and, if the truth be told, managers must acquire some of the skills of the propagandist. There are five issues:

- managers must be 100 per cent clear about their core performance standards
- only a few (not more than four) performance themes can be

followed at any one time

- managers, supervisors and workers should know exactly what the standards mean in relation to their actual tasks
- individuals should feel that they are being fairly treated, so that they will 'buy into' company standards
- an energetic and comprehensive programme of persuasive communication[2] must be continuously pursued.

Managers must realize that they communicate standards by symbolic actions – the behaviour of leaders sets the tone. No organization will do things right unless those with power practise what they preach. To be explicit, managers must indoctrinate people to do everything well, down to the smallest details like how to water the office plants. Every time that casual standards are accepted the principle of doing things right is undermined. This means that managers must become very selective about what they do. Sloppy performance cannot be tolerated so it is important to be precise about what the organization is dedicated to achieve.

The power of the concept is reflected in the sustained success of the Mars company. It has been an ethic of the company, long practised by Forest Mars, the founder, that everyone works – and is seen to work. All employees, from the managing director to the junior typist, are required to clock in and out. Laziness is almost unthinkable. A Mars manager told us: 'We are action oriented, but everyone makes damn sure that they do things really well. This is not a company that accepts a casual approach.'

As part of our research into the impact of values on company culture Dave Francis undertook a comparative study of two factories making identical products – one was in the UK and the other in the USA. Each had similar equipment, used the same ingredients, had comparable overhead costs and made the same brands of convenience foods. However, the American plant was almost twice as productive as its UK rival. Why did this enormous difference in productivity occur? Several days were spent interviewing workers at all levels, and this revealed striking differences.

The Americans demonstrated two simple attributes: professionalism and pride in the job. From floor sweeper to factory manager each employee in the American plant regarded his or her job as something to be done well. The floor sweeper did not wander around morosely, wasting every possible second. He was seen in his lunch break reading a copy of *Factory Sanitation Monthly*. This attitude was typical. Everyone interviewed showed a commitment to the job.

The British demonstrated different attitudes as they performed identical tasks. There was an air of sullen resentment in the factory. Decades of aggressive trade union defensiveness had left its mark on management-union relationships. Management saw the workforce as intransigent mules who needed coercion, whilst the workforce acted as if they were the victims of relentless exploitation. Many errors occurred through indifference and neglect. The cost was seen in the productivity figures. A postscript to this story is that the British factory has now closed.

We learn from this story that doing things right is an aspect of company culture – the system of values, beliefs, practices, attitudes and habits which give an organization its special character. Accordingly, management have to manage (not be managed by) the key dimensions of company culture by:

- ensuring that managers share a common view of the organization's direction
- awakening everyone to the nature of those competitive forces which are threats
- monitoring values and beliefs at every level
- putting money into climate change programmes
- making a senior manager responsible for integrating climate change activities.

It comes as a shock when we observe that those organizations which insist on high standards enjoy a well-motivated workforce. Many, perhaps most, people like to associate themselves with excellence and it becomes a source of personal pride. Care must be taken to ensure that the same standards are attained by all hierarchical levels. Gone are the days when the bosses could live a life of indolence, whilst employees are expected to behave like docile worker bees. The 'doing things right' ethic must apply from top to bottom.

There are five benefits of a 'doing things right' culture:

1 Increased probability that corporate strategies will be successfully implemented.
2 Easier integration of new technologies.
3 Fewer damaging interdepartmental conflicts.
4 More chance that employees will be 'positive'.
5 Higher customer satisfaction.

Practical ways to do things right have been developed over the past decade. An example makes the point. At the work group level, many organizations now use the Quality Circles approach. Almost everyone is impressed when they attend a Quality Circles meeting for the first time. A group of workers meet, under the guidance of the supervisor, to discuss concrete proposals for improving operations in the department. The enthusiasm is infectious. Apparently small matters, like the layout of components, are analyzed, discussed and brainstormed. Detailed proposals emerge, and many of the ideas prove sound.

Quality Circles are not a magic solution. It takes a great deal of work to get the approach to work. Nevertheless, we need such concepts for rebuilding care into the workplace. Such techniques transform good intentions into action, without undermining the power structure of the organization.

Again and again we return to the topic of 'culture'. All communities develop an identifiable character which is a system of unwritten beliefs, conventions and typical ways of behaving. New recruits absorb the prevailing values through the process of socialization. The individuals may change, but the culture lives on – almost as if the organization is a living thing. The behaviours which encourage a 'doing things right' culture include:

- management practising what they preach
- restructuring organizations into smaller units, to increase the sense of ownership
- getting as many employees as possible to have contact with customers, so that they feel the impact of their work on others
- reviewing the reward system to support the 'doing things right' ethic
- giving 'saturation' training to inculcate the desired values
- using high involvement techniques, like Quality Circles, to channel interest, tap creativity, increase care and heighten commitment
- establishing clear success criteria and monitoring performance.

Planned programmes to change organizational cultures can have two enemies: cynicism from the bulk of employees, and inadequate skills of managers. Most people who work in organizations have witnessed many attempts to enliven and focus corporate energies. Inevitably they go along with the latest enthusiasms but bide their time inwardly, knowing that next month a new fad will emerge. The antidote to cynicism is dedicated managers who have committed themselves to change and have the skills to lead a change programme. Superficial pronouncements of good intentions make a negative impact. It is necessary to identify a few profound principles and hammer them home continuously. When actions support words people begin to feel that 'this is for real' and, slowly, cynicism dissipates.

All these thoughts occurred to us as we suffered that irritating flight. When the plane was somewhere over Greenland we asked ourselves what we would do if it was our airline that was comprehensively mistreating us. We decided that there were four policies which we would adopt and monitor with aggressive intensity.

1   Comprehensively train the leading flight attendants as team leaders and ensure that frequent retraining occurs.
2   Insist that structured pre-flight meetings always take place so that the cabin crew are 'tuned in' to the task.
3   Collect feedback from a sample of customers on every flight, and insist that the crew discuss how to eliminate every reasonable negative observation.
4   Regularly check attitudes amongst all the cabin crew to reduce the risk that there will be a build-up of lethargy or resentment.

As we left the plane in Denver, struggling past the crew who were only concerned with their own last-minute packing, we realized, once again, that brilliant business strategic manoeuvres are a small part of the managerial job. The secret is getting thousands of simple things done well, time and time again.

Three months after we started writing this chapter on that Continental Airlines flight to New Zealand, via Denver, and after many rewrites the final editing was done by Mike on a South African Airways flight from London to Johannesburg. It was a marked contrast. Nothing was too much trouble for the cabin staff. They did *everything* right, and never stopped smiling throughout the fifteen-hour flight. Next time we have a choice about which airline to fly, the decision will be obvious! Organizations who do things right get the customers!

Summary

Core principles

- the customer is the ultimate judge of whether you 'do things right'
- people see the world in different ways, but organizations need people to perform in similar ways

- when social values do not support efficiency management must fight against the prevailing social trends
- it is necessary to influence the 'opinion leaders' at every level, as these are the people who largely determine standards
- it is possible deliberately to develop and sustain a high-performing 'culture'
- excessive bureaucracy undermines efficiency – as responsibility is taken away from the individual so quality falls
- managers must develop the skills of effective persuaders
- symbolic communication, what managers actually do, is more powerful than words
- an organization can be destroyed when 'doing things wrong' becomes part of the culture
- people take a pride in doing things well
- Quality Circles are an example of building a 'doing things right' culture into work groups
- managers must practise what they preach
- the secret is 'getting thousands of simple things done well – time and time again'.

Five steps to encourage 'doing things right'

1   Set up two study groups with membership from several levels of your organization. Assign both groups the task of examining your most successful competitors to identify what is special about their ways of doing things. The groups should work independently to avoid the risk of 'groupthink'. If possible, they should visit the other organizations and examine their products, services, policies, practices etc. They should talk to customers. Each group should then conduct a three-hour workshop for the top team on their findings and ideas on how to learn from your competitors.

2   Experiment with the Quality Circles concept in practice. Select keen and progressive middle managers and tell them to learn about the benefits and disadvantages of the application of Quality Circles. It is often helpful to involve an experienced consultant. Choose several promising work groups and apply the techniques. Carefully monitor the results. Avoid extending the use of the technique too quickly to other parts of your organization.

3   Ask your training department to obtain a copy of the film *Who Killed the Sale?*[3] (which is a superb technique for alerting people to

the issues connected with doing things right). The trainers should propose how the film (or an alternative) could be used as part of an organization-wide campaign. The discussion group technique is recommended. Experiment with the use of the film in selected parts of the organization.

4 Have a monthly 'Quality Theme' which deals with an aspect of doing things right. Everyone in the organization should be 'blitzed' with the need to deal with the particular issue. Use all the techniques of the advertising professionals. Ideas should be solicited from each level in the organization. A fully participative approach is best. Obtain feedback on the success of your communications, and keep refreshing the message.

5 Find ways for managers to learn about the topic of 'changing organizational culture'. Obtain input from academics, consultants and managers who have experienced the process first hand. There is much useful written material.[4] Experiment with techniques for measuring corporate culture. Try controlled experiments in changing culture and learn from the experience.

References

1 Max Weber, *The Protestant Ethic and the Spirit of Capitalism.*
2 See ch. 5, Dave Francis, *Unblocking Organizational Communication*, Gower, Aldershot, 1987.
3 *Who Killed the Sale?*, Rank Training, PO Box 70, Great West Road, Brentford, PW8 9HR.
4 See, for example, Edgar H. Schein, *Organizational Culture and Leadership*, Jossey-Bass, San Francisco, 1986.

8 Economy: No free lunches

It is a great deal easier to spend money than to make it. Lack of effective cost control is a common cause of business failure and organizational waste. The discipline of the profit and loss account gives commercial enterprises the ultimate measure of success. Every activity costs money; someone, somewhere has to pay. Successful managers understand the importance of economic reality and that 'there is no such thing as a free lunch'. They adopt the value: *no free lunches.*

The entrepreneurs of the nineteenth century concerned themselves with old-fashioned virtues like balanced books, low borrowing and 'real' money. They asserted that everything had to be earned, or, to borrow Milton Friedman's expressive phrase, 'There is no such thing as a free lunch'.

This prudent philosophy was deemed by many influential people to be obsolete by the 1950s, when many influential decision makers became guided by the economic theories of John Maynard Keynes, one of the most original thinkers of the twentieth century. His prescriptions for national wellbeing included spending one's way out of recession and stimulating economic activity by increasing consumption. Many economies implemented variants of Keynesian theory but experienced major problems, especially rampant inflation.

In recent years we have seen the rise of alternative economic theories, which seek to remedy the practical weaknesses of Keynesian theory.

Many of them owe their origins to the ideas of Adam Smith who wrote in 1776:[1]

> . . . every individual necessarily labours to render the annual revenue of the society as great as he can. He generally, indeed, neither intends to promote the public interest, nor knows he is promoting it . . . he intends only his own gain, and he is in this as in many other cases, led by an invisible hand to promote an end that was no part of his intention. By pursuing his own interest he frequently promotes that of the society more effectually than when he really intends to promote it.

Adam Smith believed that when people freely pursue self-interest they in fact contribute to national wellbeing. This economic viewpoint has been re-enlivened in the last twenty years, especially by the economist Milton Friedman, whose intellectual wisdom inspired managers in the 1970s to rediscover the fundamental truth in Mr Micawber's dictum: 'Annual income twenty pounds, annual expenditure nineteen pounds six, result happiness. Annual income twenty pounds, annual expenditure twenty pounds, nought and six, result misery'.

What has this to do with management? Of course, managers do not have to understand macro-economics in detail. But their own economic theories affect their day-to-day decision making. An economic theory is a crucial part of the managerial value system.

The change in the prevailing economic philosophy from Keynesian to monetarist is a partial return to traditional prudent economic precepts, and it has influenced managers in several important ways.

Most of today's senior managers studied economics in the 1940s–1960s and were greatly influenced by the Keynesian tradition. Perhaps more importantly, in many countries they are (or were), in part, victims of government economic policies, which are profligate. The 'softness' of Keynesianism enables an appeasing industrial relations ethos to thrive. For example, in the 1970s British management found itself unable to take prudent action, partly as a result of government-inspired spendthrift mentality.

Managers have been disadvantaged over the long term by the Keynesian economic stance which undermines the belief that we should only pay ourselves what we deserve and only spend what we earn. Unfortunately, a view of economics developed which suggested that 'they' could make the world prosperous simply by printing more money. This led to an unwarranted belief in the power of government and a lack of concern with the fundamental principle that it can only be profit and loss accounts that measure commercial success.

The consequences of neglecting economic reality are well illustrated by a personal example. Some years ago, both of the authors worked with an industrial training board whose task was to encourage the development of human resources across a wide spectrum of British companies. We devoted ourselves with energy and enthusiasm, but only after Dave left this now defunct government agency to build his own business did he realize just how much money had been foolishly spent in trying to achieve training board objectives. Mike, an accountant and businessman, had constantly argued for economic prudence, but was rarely heard. It was a routine occurrence to call people from all over the country for lengthy meetings, money was readily spent on staying in elegant hotels and, of course, there was the usual annual scramble to spend surplus funds before the end of the financial year. In our work with the training board we probably took hundreds of direct and indirect decisions to spend money which, if the cash had been ours, we would not have done. This was not a deliberately prodigal approach; indeed from some viewpoints we were commendably careful, but the whole organization was driven by concerns other than value for money.

Such wasteful attitudes are often found in organizations which spend other people's money. They do not think about Milton Friedman's insight that 'there is no such thing as a free lunch', nor do they consider that when they spend so easily they are diverting resources away from wealth creation.

One senior manager (responsible for a large company in New Zealand) put the matter clearly. She said: 'The plain truth is that, whether we like it or not, we have to live and compete in world markets. Our national standard of living is dependent upon economic performance. In the end people will always choose to buy that which offers the best value for money, and it follows that those companies or countries which do not offer value for money will fail to prosper.' This simple but profound argument must be universally appreciated.

The wisdom of this simple analysis is illustrated by a study of the British economy throughout the 1970s. Wages rose faster than output and thus fuelled inflation. This increased the cost of goods and services and the nation became increasingly uncompetitive. Industries in other countries took advantage of the weakness in the British economy and, as a direct result, unemployment grew in the United Kingdom. With much pain and upheaval a large number of British firms went out of business. To mix our metaphors, all those free lunches came home to roost.

Managers, perhaps more than most categories of people, must clarify their own values about economics. Government has a guiding hand. In the 1980s many governments, including the Soviet Union, began to expose their industries to the shock of global commercial realities. There was a partial return to the values of a free market economy. Where this has been done, for example in the United Kingdom, for the first time in many years productivity began to improve very significantly. The organizations which have adapted and survived are genuinely 'leaner and fitter'. Twenty years of trying to be competitive through negotiation had largely failed. Direct exposure to the tyranny of the profit and loss account was much more successful.

It is a fundamental belief of successful managements' thinking that companies perform better when they are exposed to the forces of free competition. This discipline is irreplaceable.

Protectionism breeds weakness. An amusing example of this occurred when some large trade unions stopped using their 'tied' printers because they were simply uncompetitive; other printers could do the job faster, better and cheaper. There are many such examples; refuse collection has become privatized in many local authorities, often reducing the cost dramatically. Even the threat of privatization often provokes greater economies.

Commercial companies must be exposed to the principle of survival of the fittest. Such enterprises welcome the invigorating discipline of the capitalist economic system, which serves as a constant reminder that efficiency, effectiveness and results are the fundamental criteria for judging results.

The value system which underlies capitalism needs to be translated into a competitive and enterprising culture. Managers know deep in their bones that Mr Micawber's dictum is true. People must at all times be reminded that their organizations should be 'financially sound and commercially viable'. Once preoccupation with economic viability is lost any organization becomes perilously vulnerable. As many people have found to their cost in recent years, bankrupt organizations do not survive. Human and material resources are wasted when economic logic ceases to be the primary consideration. One manager made the point this way: 'It is inhumane to manage badly or become uncompetitive. What human principle would this serve?'

An example illustrates the 'no free lunch' principle. The early months of a breakfast commercial television company, TV-am, demonstrated painfully that good ideas and a vision of the future are necessary, but not sufficient, ingredients for success. Lord Marsh, chairman of TV-am, described the first disastrous year this way:

> That was probably where we failed as a board – we hadn't appointed a management team. There are seldom any villains in this kind of thing. I think that the biggest fault of those running it initially was simply a tendency not to see TV-am as a perfectly normal business which has to have financial controls, management information, cash flow forecasts – all the dull, dreary things which at the end of the day are what you succeed or fail by.

New management had to get the basic economics right, literally by cutting out those free lunches – only then did TV-am begin to thrive. Later the new-found economic reality resulted in a highly successful flotation on the UK stock market. This success would never have been possible in the days of free lunches.

We must conclude, therefore, that for individuals, companies, industries or nations the judgement of the marketplace is what really matters.

The antidote to economic myopia is stark exposure to commercial realities. The biological analogy is perfect: without appropriate exercise and a balanced diet, human beings degenerate into flabby and unhealthy specimens. Organizations grow stronger under a tough regime. The harsh, sometimes crude, discipline of commercial results is the only strategy for survival. The principle is that the more people are protected from the economic consequences of their actions, the more their long-term future is prejudiced.

The consequences of not using this economic-realities driven management philosophy are severe. An example illustrates the point. Between the two world wars the British motorcycle industry was the world's leading producer. A British bike was a well-engineered, state-of-the-art thoroughbred offering excellent value for money. Success continued for a while after the Second World War; then Japanese manufacturers saw opportunities and swept the world market with their convenient, low-cost, excellent new-generation motorcycles. British producers initially reacted with a dogmatic rejection of the facts, claiming that the new fashions would be short-lived affairs. Then they tried to compete – sadly too little, too late. Now, the British motorcycle industry is virtually dead.

One manager friend who had worked in the British motorcycle industry put the point particularly well. He commented: 'Managers should step back from their day-to-day preoccupations and reflect upon the reasons for economic decline. What happens nationally is reflected in most organizations. It is both untruthful and wrong to blame work people alone for national weakness.' Most people now accept that both management and workers enjoyed too many 'free lunches' in the immediate postwar period. It does not pay to be soft and indulgent. In the authors' experience there are winds of change blowing through the boardrooms in many countries. Managements must take much of the blame for the lack of commercial consciousness at every organizational level.

The corrosive psychological effects of Keynesian economics will take time to wash out. A factory cleaner cannot be expected to respect the higher financial objectives of the boardroom unless these are described in ways which relate to his job and his world. What do millions of pounds, management ratios and international currency fluctuations mean to him? The true answer is 'a great deal', but too often top management fails to communicate this message effectively. The educational role is important to all managers. Messages must not be crude manipulative propaganda if they are to be credible. Persuasive communication is only effective when it is valid and truthful, but, unfortunately, managers are usually ill-trained in effective communication.

The marketplace offers an ever-present 'university' which teaches what succeeds and what fails. We may not like the lessons but they are real. Managers in successful organizations work to ensure that every member of the organization feels in contact with the marketplace. One example in Volvo who ensures that when a car is returned with significant faults the relevant production team sees the results of its poor workmanship and puts it right. Japanese businessmen talk about taking the skin temperature of the customer each day. Such market consciousness, ideally, is promoted by insightful accountants who are required to know the firm's products, not bury themselves in figures. As the chairman of a large company told us, 'the aim must be to ensure that all become acutely aware of the real implications of today's economic environment. Otherwise we will all lose.'

Economic factors are increasingly international. An illustration is the destruction of the European zip industry in the 1970s. The Japanese YKK company developed high-quality, low-cost machines which enabled them to become superb producers. They entered Europe and the existing zip manufacturing companies, once cosy in their protected havens, were virtually destroyed. This industry, like many others, realized too late that it is insufficient to be just nationally competitive. Commercial realities operate on an international scale. Of course, this has profound implications for managers, who must seek out the most competent, comparable organizations anywhere in the world, and study them with the rapt attention that a cat gives to mouse.

Management implications

At a down-to-earth level an economic preoccupation means that successful managers are committed to 'good husbandry'. Jobs are examined to discover what potential influence the individual can have over economic performance, and these variables are measured, recorded and regularly reviewed. Computer systems increasingly make it possible to give rapid feedback to job holders. Even in non-commercial fields this can be done. For example, in many countries doctors get feedback on the costs involved in meeting their prescriptions for drugs, and can use this information to give value for money.

Unfortunately, measurements and feedback are often the responsibility of 'experts' who, in our experience, are usually primarily concerned with meeting legal and system requirements. So they fail to contribute fully their professional skills to increasing commercial awareness and promoting better systems for giving key financial data to those who can use the information. After all, the only good reason for reviewing the past is to change future behaviour. Specialists are often perceived as necessary but jaundiced sceptics obsessively concerned with their own routines.

Although commercial success is fundamental, it is not always supreme. Sometimes more important principles are at stake. Many countries are applying sanctions against South Africa against their own commercial interests and many governments and organizations are realizing that they have to be more conscious of environmental factors. Politics and social principles often need to override profit.

Commercial logic requires that long-term interests are not sacrificed for short-term gain. The insistent demands of monthly and annual high targets tend to focus managers' minds on the immediate, not the long term. Profitability today may disguise potential weakness tomorrow. Successful managers are committed to permanence and make prudent investments which pay off years later. They try to balance profit today with investment in the future. That contributes to the long-term benefit of shareholders, employees and the community.

Summary

Core principles

- Economic concerns values are a crucial part of the organization's value system
- managers often need to clarify their own economic values
- monetarist economic theories provide the most useful economic model for managers in commercial companies
- we should pay ourselves what we deserve and only spend what we earn
- organizations thrive best when they are children of capitalism
- governments cannot remedy all economic weaknesses
- non-commercial organizations are especially vulnerable to forgetting the 'no free lunch' principle
- every employee must be concerned with profit and loss
- direct exposure to economic reality is the best way to make an organization lean and fit
- great efforts have to be made to ensure that employees understand the economic results of their work
- jobs should be described in ways that focus on the economic consequences of success and failure
- specialist managers should receive training to help them to understand the impact of their specialism on the organization as a whole
- sometimes deeper issues, like the maintenance of law and order, override economic considerations
- long-term economic viability must be built without sacrificing short-term profitability.

Five steps to encourage the 'no free lunch' value

1 Ask each senior manager to prepare a written answer to the question: 'Imagine you owned this organization – what would you do differently?' Compile an overview of the suggestions made for top management review and action planning.

2   Arrange for your trade union representatives to receive business school training in the financial aspects of management. Ensure that they are aware of the economic impact of wage rates and labour restrictions on productivity. Find ways for them to examine competitors' finances both at home and abroad.
3   Ask every manager to identify ways in which his or her department or unit 'adds value' to products or services. These can be boldly written on a poster displayed in the workplace and constantly reviewed. Enlist the help of computer consultants to discover how you can supply more immediate and graphic information on productivity to those immediately concerned.
4   Give all supervisors and managers company/unit accounts and help them to understand the implications. If necessary special training programmes should be conducted. Then each manager or supervisor discusses the implications with members of their own teams, and they, in turn, cascade such discussions down through the organization.
5   Obtain comparative statistics on the profitability and productivity of your part of the organization compared with similar ones in the USA, Japan and Europe. (Such information is often obtainable from trade or industry associations.) Make the information widely available and discuss it across the organization. Form action groups to remedy identified weaknesses.

Reference

1   Adam Smith, *An Inquiry into the Nature and Causes of the Wealth of Nations*, edited by E. Cannam, Methuen, 1922, p. 423.

Part IV

MANAGING
RELATIONSHIPS

9 Fairness: Who cares wins

One of the greatest compliments paid to a good teacher is that he or she is firm but fair. Managements, by their actions, greatly affect people's lives, both in work and outside. What they do, and what they refuse to do, has a great impact on the quality of life of their subordinates. The use of this power with compassion and fairness builds trust and commitment. Successful managers realize that people's views, perceptions and feelings are important. They adopt the value: *who cares wins*.

Throughout the centuries enlightened businessmen and women have accepted a moral responsibility to run organizations in ways that enable individuals to thrive. Managerial power shapes the destiny of all those who work in the organization and the most successful industrialists care for both people and profit. In the early twentieth century this stance evolved into a definite management philosophy, known as 'paternalism', which advocates that those in control of organizations should behave like good fathers.

Paternalism was not to last. After the Second World War, coincidental with the expansion of trade union power and the welfare state, paternalism became derided as a wasteful and soft-headed philosophy which disregarded current realities and was considered to be essentially humiliating to employees.

Paternalism is 'the principle and practice of paternal administration: government as by a father' (*Shorter Oxford Dictionary*). There are, of course, many variations of the paternal role. The proper role of a father is to provide whatever is needed to bring the child to responsible adulthood. This requires firmness and understanding, discipline and freedom. Fathers give both support and direction. In return, they gain loyalty and love.

It is a shame that paternalism became so unfashionable. For years after the Second World War in many countries trade unions attracted almost unquestioned loyalty and many employers were cast in the role of the enemy. Such social divisions proved very destructive. Workers are usually dependent upon the organization that employs them. Their lives are greatly influenced by decisions taken far above them. What is wrong with decision makers recognizing that they are partly responsible for the interests of their employees?

Let us take the argument further by considering how managerial power is used. All large organizations centralize strategic decision making into the hands of relatively few people who become an elite. Top managers can devise effective systems for collecting information, making choices and allocating resources. Most commercial organizations in the Western World use ownership as the principle on which power is distributed. Non-commercial organizations (like local government) use democratically elected groups to perform the same role. Whatever approach is used the result is the same; a small group directs the fortunes of the whole. The ruling elite invariably operates with an explicit or implicit code of morality or immorality.

Some top managements, from our observation, pay scant attention to their paternal responsibilities, yet they take considerable care in technical analysis. Markets are studied, graphs drawn, strategies evaluated and opportunities carefully weighed. A considerable amount of expertise is invested in strategic decisions, but little time is spent on considering human issues. Such top managers take every possible precaution to avoid undue risks. They try to invest in ventures with a high probability of profit. But emphasis on short-term return on investment to the exclusion of other criteria is contrary to the principles of paternalism. Human interests, beginning with material prosperity, are the primary goals. As we have said many times throughout this book, mere materialism is a shallow philosophy.

Once managers begin to consider the morality of their decisions they almost always move to becoming more paternalistic. The best of them show enormous care for their employees but are never 'soft'. Paternalism requires surveillance and watchfulness. Employees are helped and guided to improve their performance. Demands are made and standards set. Increasing competence earns increasing recognition. The main danger for paternalistic managers is that they can get out of touch. They assume that they know what is good for others and communication difficulties often occur. Such problems are not inevitable. If the right degree of watchfulness is maintained then paternalism does not have to result in psychological isolation.

Behaving like a good father may seem opposed to the principles of individualism and self-reliance. Not so! The individual freely decides that he or she will strike a bargain with an employer. Organizations, in effect, then demand that employees abandon some of the responsibility for their own destiny but individual workers have made a free choice to put their wellbeing partly in the hands of someone else. Once this decision is made the individual has invested in the fortunes of a corporate body and has a right to expect that this trust will be reciprocated.

Fortunately, paternalism is not dead. It is undergoing a renaissance and has risen again under different guises. For example, many American companies have instituted a policy of social responsibility. Leading Japanese firms, who are teaching us much about the effective use of resources, adopt employee philosophies which support the individual through thick and thin. Many European companies are reflecting anew on business ethics. This is a new-style paternalism which accepts that organizations have a moral responsibility for the consequences of managerial decisions.

It is difficult to capture in words the subtle blend of boldness and caution which typifies the caring stance. For an explanation we can borrow an idea from a great industrialist. Thomas Watson of IBM recognized the fundamental importance of solid beliefs in organizational success. He wrote:[1]

Consider any great organization that has lasted over the years, and I think you will find that it owed its resilience not to its form of organization or administrative skills, but to the power of what we call beliefs and the appeal these beliefs provide. This, then, is my thesis: I firmly believe that any organization, in order to survive and achieve success must have a sound set of beliefs on which it premises all its policies and actions. Next, I believe that the most important single factor in the corporate success is faithful adherence to those beliefs.

And finally, I believe that if an organization is to meet the challenges of a changing world, it must be prepared to change everything about itself except those beliefs as it moves through corporate life.

A number of industrialists have understood the importance of moral leadership. Sir John Egan described his period as managing director of Jaguar Cars in the following way: 'Overall we have tried to create an environment at Jaguar which is the exact opposite of the purely instrumental approach which characterizes the employee's attitude to his company in so much of industry. We know the dividends this pays, not only in terms of generating a much better atmosphere within our factories but also in our people's willingness to go far beyond the normal call of duty when problems arise.' The Jaguar approach paid off – productivity trebled between 1980 and 1984 and industrial stoppages fell from 800,000 employee hours to less than 5,000 hours.[2]

Opponents claim that paternalism inevitably generates dependency, and so damages personal initiative and self-responsibility. Moreover, it is argued that paternalism is expensive and leads to an unacceptable tolerance of inefficiency. The anti-paternalists argue that fair wages are sufficient reward for effort and that providing more erodes managerial discretion, blunts the competitive edge and binds workers to organizations for negative reasons.

Paternalism is a hazardous management philosophy because it can degenerate into a soft and weak stance if the commitment to high standards is lacking. That which is given from an enlightened and compassionate attitute may be seen as 'something for nothing'. If they support unacceptable behaviour managers store up trouble ahead. However, if the tightrope can be walked then paternalism is positive and morally defensible and justifies a relentless drive towards productivity.

Well managed paternalism evokes loyalty. Some of the most successful organizations thrive because they possess a strong ideology which includes a caring philosophy towards people. This may arise from the vision of one person; alternatively such loyalty can grow slowly as episodes of distinguished endeavour amass into a historic identity.

Caring like a good father also has implications for the role business plays in the wider community. In an address to the Institute of Directors the Prince of Wales once drew attention to a neglected facet of business values – responsibility to the community as a whole. Prince Charles pointed out that business naturally exploited 'rich pickings' and so neglected the poorer areas of society. This meant that socially deprived areas degenerated further, both materially and morally. Large companies tended to suck wealth out of rundown communities and give little in return. He argued that owners and managers should maintain financial viability but use part of their power and wealth with the attitude of a good parent to help society as a whole. Such philanthropic attitudes are part of the caring tradition. They are not pie in the sky either. For example, in Brixton, South London, new community enterprises are thriving, funded in part by big business. In Mike Woodcock's constituency of Ellesmere Port many new businesses have been helped to grow by assistance from large established firms. Much more, however, needs to be done.

Caring management

The rediscovery of caring principles is fashionable in the USA, where some management opinion leaders have discovered the importance of 'meaning' and 'purpose'. They describe the need for organizations to have a 'heart' and express human values. Purely rational strategies and concentration on profit are seen as necessary, but insufficient, motivators. Instead organizations should be regarded as growing organisms which need a clear sense of purpose. Such management philosophies are greeted as novel and extraordinary, but are really updated variations of paternalistic themes which have long been understood by the best industrialists and leaders.

Managers who deliberately lack principles are operating on the principle that they have no principles – if you see what we mean. Organizations likewise operate from principles whether these have been articulated or not. They trade in certain ways and not others, treat their employees according to a definite philosophy, and promote some activities rather than others.

A coherent set of principles is a source of strength because:

- decisions are firmer
- a consistent approach is adopted
- issues can be judged more quickly
- important 'crunch points' can be readily identified
- others respect a principled stance
- trust is built.

Those who manage without a sound foundation of principles are weak or untrustworthy. In a crisis the unprincipled person tends to react to immediate pressures and to make bad decisions which have ramifications for years to come.

Principles can be clarified by these four steps:

1 *Decide to be honest.* Only by examining how you really think and feel (not how you 'should') can genuine principles be uncovered.
2 *Express your current views.* Allowing yourself to express your views freely reveals what your stance really is.
3 *Consider alternatives.* Develop the capacity to open your mind to other views.
4 *Write down your principles.* This helps you clarify and, equally important, test whether your principles are consistent with each other.

Often people say one thing and do another. Such inconsistency is important, and should be explored. The way you actually behave is a more lucid statement of your principles than your rhetoric.

It is often helpful to discuss and debate principles with others. Reasonable and factual argument is a great antidote to prejudice and bigotry. Moreover, it is valuable to gather viewpoints from people whose stance is very different from your own.

Caring managers know their principles and seek to put them into effect. This is difficult as principles are ephemeral things, difficult to grasp and hard to consider. As managers discuss their principles about people they can find themselves mouthing high-sounding phrases which they never practise. Somehow such discussions awake half-remembered sermons from school assemblies. Principles must be simple, explicit and then driven home.

John Harvey-Jones, ex-chairman of ICI, believes that the most effective organizations are those in which the values of the organization support the values of the individual and vice versa. He said: 'You cannot, in industry, work totally on the principle that the end justifies the means. The ends have to be felt to be good and the ethics of the organization, i.e. how it behaves in pursuit of its ends, have to be seen as decent and in tune with the times.' Harvey-Jones was amazed that 'ethics' was only an optional extra at the Harvard Business School.[3] Business schools have traditionally paid scant regard to ethics, values and principles. If these topics are not seriously studied in the upper echelons of business education it is not surprising that few senior managers can describe a coherent set of caring principles.

Many organizations of the left, for example, the Co-operative movement, have a distinguished record of implementing paternalistic policies if not of commercial success. The distinctive element of productive paternalism is the 'contractual' principle on which it is based. Expressed simply this says: 'We will care for you if you give us what we want!' Paternalism should be demanding as well as giving.

The right-wing view of paternalism is akin to that of the good father whose support is strong but conditional – the child is cared for within limits but encouraged to take responsibility for himself whenever possible. The socialist concept of paternalism is more like that of the mother, with unconditional support no matter what the child does. We accept that total care for infants is both necessary and desirable. Adults, however, thrive poorly in totally benign environments. Personal initiative needs to be developed and withers without use. Accounts of prison camps vividly illustrate that prisoners' capacity to make decisions deteriorates if it cannot be used. Mothering of adults is a stultifying process which erodes individual dignity.

Managers must be realists; they know that many people develop a degree of dependence on their employer, which often suits managers who require most employees to play significant but highly limited roles. Dependency is a dangerous relationship for the dependent person. There is a strong probability that people will find themselves in difficulties. Illness or family problems occur and, most common these days, jobs are radically changed or rendered obsolete. Top managers in a large conglomerate may decide to restructure a nationwide business and a small dot on the map, representing a branch office, is removed. This is a relatively trivial matter for executives, but has dramatic consequences for those affected.

The roles of 'father' and 'mother' carry powerful emotional undertones. The paternal figure often triggers hostile reactions. Traditional authoritarian behaviour tends to evoke childlike responses like passive compliance or loud aggressive resistance. Neither is constructive. 'Acting superior' with a judgmental and punitive style is often provocative. The manner of expression is as significant as the content.

Despite the difficulties of expression we cannot avoid observing that great organizations are often led by caring managers who are great paternalists. They succeed because their employees work well for them. The best situation for managers is to have a fiercely loyal and high-performing workforce. Managements gain points by helping those who are disadvantaged, rewarding loyalty, enriching the quality of working life and doing everything possible to be 'good employers'.

As part of our preparation for this book we asked twenty-three long-established chairmen of successful companies about their decision-making styles, and some common features emerged:

- ensuring that they have an objective assessment of the strengths and weaknesses of their own businesses
- clarifying what factors give the organization its distinctive character
- finding out what members of the organization feel proud of achieving
- encouraging objective analysis and critique of the present organization
- demonstrating that they are prepared to listen
- honouring the history of their organization
- seeking out and 'unblocking' areas of the organization which have degenerated
- exercising caution in introducing new ideas
- explaining fully their reasoning on important decisions
- avoiding looking down on the workforce.

A 'bargain' is the essence of the paternal relationship. Lord Bancroft, former head of the UK Civil Service, helped us understand the fundamental importance of a contract between management and staff. He said: 'A management's deeds and words should approximate to each other. It is all very well to tell staff that management will strike a bargain; that in return for efficiency, effectiveness and economy it will encourage and care for its employees. Both sides must keep to any implicit or explicit bargain.' Books on childcare tell us that the young require consistency from their parents: employees are entitled to expect integrity from their bosses.

Benefits of paternalism

Paternalism can be supported for six reasons:

- organizations earn high commitment from employees by showing high commitment to them
- managements' 'right to manage' is enhanced by an obviously responsible stance

- people are more likely to trust a 'good' employer
- in a competitive job market respected employers attract the best recruits
- managers feel more able to take a 'surgical' approach to managing change if they know possible damage to people will be minimized
- paternalism undermines destructive class barriers and weakens the power base of militant trade unions.

New style paternalism is clearly different from the pompous superiority often shown by the Victorian mill owner. It is persuasive rather than oppressive. All possible mechanisms for persuasion are used to communicate with the workforce. There is an interesting analogy with computers which have, in recent years, become 'user-friendly'. This means that the computer is approachable, communicates in language that the user can understand and appears to adopt a considerate attitude. Managements are learning to become user-friendly in the same way. This does not reduce the paternal responsibilities of management, but it changes the form of expression to one in keeping with our age.

An additional dimension of caring is concern for stable human communities. Organizations depend on communities and people depend on organizations: the relationship is 'mutual interdependence'. Managers can support communities in several ways:

- direct economic support – through gifts, endowments, sponsorships, trusts etc.
- indirect economic support – by encouraging wealth creation
- managerial support – by giving brainpower and expertise to community programmes
- educational support – by allowing the organization to welcome and help students and visitors
- political support – by encouraging and funding political representatives whose philosophy is congenial
- resource support – by assisting in community projects by donating resources.

Caring managers have a tradition of being community-oriented; a proportion of corporate wealth is often allocated to community benefit. They take care to see that expenditure of time and money is afforded as 'businesses can only be responsible if they are profitable'. Yet managers must ask: 'Profit for what?' One colleague put it this way: 'pursuing profit for its own sake is rooted in the shallow motivation of a miser, and gives a woefully inadequate base to build successful organizations. Profitability is the primary goal as it permits people to lead lives with choice and richness, but it is not an end in itself.'

A company chairman who built a large and successful enterprise disclosed his personal philosophy with great candour. He said: 'I feel a commitment to my organization which is akin to love. I have a great regard for the business and the people who work there. I am unwilling to be parted from my organization, and I feel a great pride in its achievements. I have been accused of being addicted to my company. The depth of emotion I feel has never been a weakness as people respond. I believe that organizations need a heart and I am prepared to play this role.' This man's view may seem naive and old-fashioned but, in fact, it is ahead of its time. Feeling and 'heart' are keys to successful management.

Summary

Core principles

- paternalistic approaches have been wrongly condemned as 'old fashioned'
- American 'social responsibility' and Japanese employee policies have much to teach European managers
- organizations which demand high productivity and loyalty look after employees in return
- paternalism should be conditional and demanding, not soft and all-embracing
- managers who skilfully adopt paternalistic attitudes are enhancing their right to manage
- many highly effective and profitable companies thrive on a policy of paternalism
- paternalism must not be expressed as crude authoritarianism
- managements must become more skilful at demonstrating the benefits of a 'high give/high take' relationship.

Five steps to encourage caring management

1 Visit some Japanese organizations and talk to the work-people about how management operates. Compare and contrast their attitudes with your own. Produce a report for top management

discussion, and set up working parties to progress any changes which seem desirable.

2 Write down how you personally would like to be treated as an employee in any organization. Then see whether those conditions are operating in your organization. Identify gaps, and forcefully bring these to the attention of those who can take action.

3 Invite an industrial psychologist who specializes in attitude surveys to give you a presentation on methods of collecting valid data on employee attitudes. Consider collecting such information regularly to find out how employees view the management of your organization. Alternatively, use the Blockage Survey[4] which is a systematic way of collecting valuable data about how an organization is functioning.

4 Informally discuss your managerial stance towards people with trade union officials. Encourage study of trade union literature by your senior managers. Obtain trade union viewpoints and use these to challenge your thinking. Keep in touch with evolving thinking in powerful rival institutions.

5 Collect together discussion groups of five employees chosen at random and invite them to discuss whether the company is a good employer. Tape record the discussion (with permission) and use the resulting analysis to encourage top management to debate whether the company is too soft, or too hard.

References

1 Thomas J. Watson Jr, *A Business and Its Beliefs: The Ideas That Helped Build IBM*, McGraw Hill, New York, 1963, p 5

2 *Personnel Management*, April 1984, p. 9.

3 Ibid., p. 10.

4 Mike Woodcock and Dave Francis, *Unblocking Your Organization*, Gower, Aldershot, 1990.

10 Teamwork: Pulling together

A well organized and motivated group can achieve more than the sum of the individuals who comprise it. People enjoy the company of others and can work well collectively. One person's talents balance the weaknesses of another. It is vitally important that people feel they belong. Successful managers ensure that they reap the benefits of effective teamwork. They adopt the value: *pulling together.*

Studies of excellent organizations capture the imagination of managers. Case studies given at expensive seminars attempt to encapsulate the attributes of the best. Over the years we have attended many such presentations on the nature of corporate excellence and can now reliably predict what will be said:

Outstanding organizations are dynamic, energetic, focused, wisely led and opportunistic. The people who work in them care about the quality of their work. There is a quality of optimism, commitment and high energy. Such organizations will change everything but their basic values. High achievement, the pursuit of excellence, is programmed into minds of employees.

All excellent organizations are the same, whether they are selling hamburgers or gathering taxes. Their success recipes are predictable but ephemeral. One other human institution shares many of the characteristics of the high performing organizations: the family. The best organizations engender the same positive qualities that close and happy families enjoy. We advocate that organizations should seek to incor-porate the value of 'family life', thereby providing a structure on which to build constructive human relationships.

Tolstoy said: 'All happy families resemble one another, but each unhappy family is unhappy in its own way'; emphasizing that the well-conducted families, like excellent organizations, are good at getting the basics right.

It is interesting that senior managers often think about their organi-zation as an extension of their own family. Clinical and dispassionate attitudes are uncharacteristic of great leaders. Families are the enduring units in human society. They provide roots which connect people with past and future. Families give identity and support. At their best they are loved and loyally protected. Of course, we must not be excessively romantic. Some families are disturbed, unhappy, tyrannical and damaging. However, few people would disagree that a soundly-based family is a powerful source for the good.

Promoting family life is an age old value. Our forefathers saw the family as an honourable and indispensable unit of society. They were cautious about tampering with such a natural phenomenon.

In the twentieth century the institution of the family has been under threat. For example, the communist movement in Russia was influenced by Marx's condemnation of the family which he believed to be an embodiment of the vices of the exploiting class. The rise of feminism, stimulated by books such as *The Feminine Mystique*,[1] accelerated the growing rebellion against traditional family form. Radicals of various persuasions advocated the demise of the family. The influential psychiatrist, R.D. Laing, saw the family as the seed bed of pathological and mental illness.[2] We disagree, believing that close-ness, kinship, support, honesty, loyalty are all attributes of a good family.

Some managers have been slow to recognize the great value of thinking of their organizations as family groups. For example, many regard people as mere units of labour and give scant recognition to their social and emotional needs. People themselves are aware of the import-ance of forming close bonds in small groups. They naturally form teams which act as 'work families', and these groups become very important in their lives.

Teams are powerful tools; they get men to the moon, audit complex accounts, make cinematic blockbusters and run companies. Efficient teamwork provides five great advantages:

- individual weaknesses are neutralized by others' strengths
- teamwork builds consensus and commitment
- membership is a strong motivator
- teams discipline errant members
- errors and sloppy thinking are less likely to occur.

The team approach can satisfy both individual and corporate needs. Combined talents and skills achieve success where lone individuals would fail. Also the well-devised team, like a healthy family, is an exceptional source of support and motivation. It stimulates its members to excel.

It is useful to distinguish between the types of teams commonly found in organizations and their main roles:

- *Top teams*. Provide direction, control and identity at the apex of the organization.
- *Management teams*. Devise, co-ordinate and control operational strategies and plans.
- *Project teams*. Undertake specific assignments or 'one-off' tasks.
- *Creative teams*. Pool different talents to devise innovative solutions and seize opportunities.
- *Work teams*. Communicate and co-operate to get jobs done.

One of the first demonstrations of the importance of teams came from a study conducted shortly after the Second World War when techniques of coal mining in Britain were being radically changed. New mechanized equipment made the traditional 'informal family' teamwork required by hand mining less appropriate. In the dangerous and dark underground conditions isolated miners were now asked to play fragmented new roles tending the 'long-wall' machines. In effect, their work family had been destroyed and informal communication was largely inhibited. The result was low motivation, poor morale and aggressive defensiveness. Researchers from the Tavistock Institute[3] suggested that teamwork should be re-established and, after this was done, gradually the social problems were solved.

During the 1970s some established companies experimented with new forms of work organization which attempted to encourage responsible attitudes in the belief that improved productivity would result. They argued that the routine of organizational life reduced people to machines and close relationships were destroyed by the factory system. Starved of genuine choice, it was not surprising that apathy and irresponsible behaviour flourished. Companies like United Biscuits,

General Foods and Imperial Chemical Industries tried to increase responsibility at shopfloor level. Dave Francis visited a dog food factory in 1975 owned by General Foods in Topeka, Kansas, and studied a highly productive and profitable unit that was organized largely by teams of operators led by a supervisor. Careful selection of personnel followed by intensive training enabled managers to assign almost all routine decision making to groups. Responsibility was, truly, passed to those who were close to the action and both workers and company shareholders gained.

Unfortunately, such experiments have proved the exception rather than the rule. Awareness of the importance of family life has been lost by many senior managers whose concerns are largely expressed in rows of numbers. Large organizations continue to create jobs that offer little discretion. It is not surprising that when genuine responsibility is absent, responsible behaviour is often lacking.

Although there have been many demonstrations of the value of team building it is not the panacea for solving all organizational problems. Some individuals are self-sustaining and, for them, teamwork is inappropriate. Even where teamwork is desirable, it requires an open communicating management style which not all managers are able or willing to use. Also, work families can turn against the wider organization.

Many managers are sceptical of 'management by committee' which they feel, undermines individuality and weakens responsibility. They recognize that they must exploit the potential of groups but watch for the disadvantages. Groups and committees can muddy decision making, undermine individual self-confidence and reduce people's contributions to the lowest common denominator. Unless well constructed, such groups can become satisfied with low-quality performance and waste an extraordinary amount of time in social intercourse. Some senior managers have noticed this tendency and understandably sound a note of caution about teamwork. For example, Peter Walters, as the Chairman of BP, speaking of the team approach, says: 'That was just one part of the personnel management claptrap which became the vogue in the 1960s. The truth was that one chap set the tone.'[4]

Ironically, the strengths of family relationships mean that a team approach has proved a source of weakness in senior decision making. Some ideas, which we introduced in Chapter 6, developed by Professor Janus,[5] are relevant here. In a provocative study, he found that some team decisions are outstandingly successful but, unfortunately, there are many examples of collective decision making which proved disastrous. His analysis of famous fiascos revealed that the team responsible committed one or more of the following blunders:

- their discussions did not survey all of the available options
- the original decision was not re-evaluated for non-obvious drawbacks
- discarded options were not re-examined for non-obvious gains
- expertise was ignored because of bias of powerful group members
- insufficient consideration was given to the reaction of outside groups.

Teams which operate like close and cohesive families are liable to commit such blunders. The group develops an isolated approach and becomes a law unto itself. This is the 'groupthink' phenomenon referred to earlier. The symptoms are:

- illusion of invulnerability feeds excessive optimism
- warnings are discounted
- ethical standards slip as the group becomes judge and jury
- other groups are considered inferior
- self-censorship prevents the expression of critical opinions within the team
- adverse information is ignored as it might shatter illusions.

The best teams are motivating and resourceful but leaders have to take care to avoid the dangers of 'groupthink'. This requires that:

- a norm is established in the group of supporting, rather than punishing, divergent comments
- systematic decision-making disciplines are understood and rigorously applied
- outside views are collected to provide a check on the validity of decision making.

The authors' experience confirms Professor Janus' analysis. Underdeveloped teams are managerially incompetent and even developed teams must be used with care. Yet over the past decade we have become increasingly aware of the flexibility and power of the family-style team.

When teams have been carefully selected, insightfully led and deliberately developed they are a force for good. The value of the team approach is emphasized for top management by the Institute of Directors who say:[6]

Although a private company may, in law, have one director only, it would be in general unwise to do so. The reason for this lies in the nature of the decisions directors take. Based as they are on uncertain assumptions about the future, they require the exercise of a great deal of judgement and mental weighing and testing. No more efficient method has yet been discovered for carrying out this process than discussion by a well-informed small group.

One is reminded of a family group discussing an important problem together and collectively coming to a resolution.

Managers are well advised to remember that people must feel a sense of ownership in their environment. One only has to walk through a production facility at Christmas time to see the hundreds of cards and messages that workers exchange. These are often festooned around the machines. People like and need to make their mark on, and possess, a small piece of the world around them.

This can be facilitated by:

- asking people what they think about their working environment
- acting to make appropriate changes in the working environment
- providing the opportunity for each person to have some personal space
- trying to humanize and individualize the environment (i.e. not allowing clinical minded designers to go unquestioned)
- trying to ensure that people feel ownership of what they produce (through personal identification).

Team construction

Over the past decade managers have realized that it is both practical and desirable deliberately to select and build effective teams. Both the authors have published practical guides to team building[7] which describe how a disparate collection of individuals can learn to operate as a cohesive and effective team.

The initial challenge is to choose the appropriate ingredients. Like a good cook the team designer uses a planned approach to find the best balance of personal skills and professional disciplines.

Some brilliant research by British management developer Meredith Belbin[8] helps us understand how to construct a successful team. Teamwork requires a careful blend of ingredients. Simplifying Dr

Belbin's analysis we find that effective teams have people capable of performing the following roles:

- 'Mr Dutiful', who works for the good of the company, is conservative and predictable
- 'Mr Chairman', who sets objectives and exploits everyone's best abilities
- 'Mr Get-up-and-go', who challenges, drives and stimulates
- 'Mr Ideas', who uses imagination and proposes new ways to get things done
- 'Mr Fix-it', who knows people and explores situations
- 'Mr Ponder', who carefully weighs options before judging
- 'Mr Harmony', who bridges differences and makes people feel at home
- 'Mr Get-the-job-done-right', who ensures that tasks are finished to a high standard.

(Of course it is not implied that all or any of these roles can be played only by men.)

The successful manager will take great care to collect a full mix of individuals in a well-balanced team. This provides a durable resource of stimulating and energetic people who complement each other's differences. Slowly, through a deliberate process of team building, they become a work family.

Team building

Steps should be taken to weld the disparate group of individuals into a close working group. This requires:

1 A team manager who wishes to use a team approach.
2 A group with objectives which require them to work together.
3 Basic willingness and skills for team working.

When these conditions are present the group is a suitable case for team building. Work relationships and 'real life' performance of tasks must be addressed, and team building focuses on improving operational performance.

Just as families thrive on openness, so team building requires that each team member 'stands back' and frankly evaluates how the team is operating as a working family. Inevitably shortcomings will be exposed, so the team manager, like anyone in a parent role, is in a vulnerable position. Much team building takes place informally, but we have found it is often helpful to have a two- or three-day team meeting devoted to improving performance. It takes leadership courage to begin. The team manager must understand what is about to happen and agree to the process.

Managers sometimes use the services of a team-building consultant as an adviser to the whole team (not just the team manager). This helps identify blockages to effectiveness, specify roles, review current practice and plan how to improve. Just as families get 'locked into' the status quo, so work teams can become insular. To offset this tendency team builders often conduct a private 'sensing interview' with each member of the team. This typically lasts for about one-and-a-half hours. What is said is considered anonymous but not confidential. Copious notes are taken, often of verbatim quotations. The consultant methodically collects data on such matters as: values of the team, its mission in the organization, goal clarity and commitment, relationships and accountability, decision-making processes and communication, leadership style and rewards, openness and trust, co-operation and competition, relationships with other teams.

Recurrent themes always emerge. The consultant can use the experience to identify and categorize data under relevant headings. Care must be taken to ensure that comments cannot be traced to the person who made them. No attempt is made to interpret the results; the consultant's only task is to accurately present a 'snapshot' of the team.

Categorized data is then presented to the team manager in a private coaching session. Several hours of discussion are usually required for the team manager to absorb the data and plan how to use it. The team-building session which follows is led by the existing team manager (not by the consultant as this would undermine the integrity of the 'family'). It is imperative that the team manager adopts a constructive role. Extensive discussion of the issues and guidance from the consultant enables the team-building session to be properly planned and conducted.

All team members then meet off-site. A country hotel is ideal as it provokes the development of family-style relationships. We have found that a useful time frame is for team building to begin after work one evening and conclude at dinner time on the third day. This allows two complete days of work, which is usually necessary for an adequate review of team functioning.

The off-site meeting can begin with an introduction by the team manager, who invites the consultant to share the data from the sensing interviews. All the information should be pre-written up on flip charts under appropriate headings. The consultant clarifies comments as he or she knew the context in which they were said. At this stage the team absorbs the information. When the consultant has finished displaying the data the leader resumes charge of the meeting and, in co-operation with other members of the team, prepares an agenda. Normally this occupies the first evening.

The subsequent two days are spent working methodically through the agenda. The team leader manages the sessions and action points emerge. These are recorded with responsibilities allocated. The consultant's task is to help the team to address issues, to direct attention to how it is operating, to give short inputs on concepts or techniques and to suggest mechanisms for improvement. Care must always be taken to ensure that the integrity of the work family is never undermined.

At the end of the session the team has reviewed its operating effectiveness and devised an action plan for improvement. By addressing practical problems and opportunities in a new collaborative manner the team evolves as a family work group, and becomes a more competent resource. It creatively devises new ways of working together in the future.

Just as families need to be sustained so do teams. It often proves helpful to hold a review session a few weeks after the off-site meeting. This enables the process to be continued, action steps to be reviewed and further development to be planned.

Because work families are devices for production they must address very specific questions. The following checklist is useful.

Effective work methods

Does everyone clearly understand the role of the team?
Are time scales explicit?
Does everyone have distinct tasks?
Are there crystal clear targets to aim for?
Are the tasks and people well organized?
Are members aware of the commercial context of their objectives?
Have individual targets been clearly set?
Is performance being properly monitored?
Are there careful and regular reviews of progress?

Is there a detailed action plan, with bench marks?

Strong leadership and control

Has the team been carefully briefed?
Does the leader demonstrate skills in creating a 'productive work family'?
Is there a clearly defined hierarchy?
Is leadership allowed to change as the task changes?

Blend of skills

Are the available resources adequate?
Have team members been trained in working together?
Are team members able to perform the necessary tasks?
Do team members have complementary personality characteristics?
Are steps taken to get the best out of all members?

Positive climate

Are time scales realistic?
Is everyone totally committed?
Does everyone want to work together?
Is there total involvement?
Does the team have a wish to achieve?
Does the team believe in its capability?
Is there empathy, rather than sympathy?

Productive 'work families' are a natural way to organize. Although there are important differences, the analogy between families and teams is sufficiently close to be meaningful. Managers are well advised to think about their organizations as work families, and build teams to sustain high performance.

Summary

Core principles

• families are the building blocks of society

- people need to relate closely to others
- teams are a source of energy and commitment
- teams are relevant at every level of organization
- teams must be taught to avoid 'groupthink'
- teams should be deliberately constructed
- teams should understand and practice team building
- team consultants should work with an established methodology
- team leaders are responsible for developing their own teams.

Five steps to develop pulling together

1 Invite two or three experienced team consultants to develop proposals for your top team building. Actively consider the suggestions and choose that which appears most valuable. Then undertake a team-building exercise and review its value.
2 Look at your current procedures for selecting members of new teams. Use the Belbin analysis described in his book as an aid to getting a full blend of personalities.
3 Get your own team together for a two-hour meeting. Use a flip chart to list the answers to these three questions:

   What things do we do well as a team now?
   What should we be aiming to achieve in the future?
   What actions need to be taken by whom to improve team performance?

   At the end of the session review whether the exercise has proved successful. If the answer is 'yes', repeat it each month.
4 Close relationships are a necessary ingredient of effective teamwork. Select a team who must work well together and invite it to experiment by attending an outward-bound type experience for three–four days. Wait three months and review the results. Continue with the experiment if the results are promising.
5 Bring a video system into your next team meeting (with the prior agreement of all concerned) and record an hour of typical discussion. Replay the tape, stopping periodically for analysis, and produce a checklist of ideas for improvement. Implement the ideas and bring back the video recorder in three months' time to assess progress.

References

1 Betty Friedan, *The Feminine Mystique*, Norton, New York, 1963.
2 R.D. Laing, *The Divided Self*, Quadrangle, Chicago, 1960.
3 E.L. Trist and K.W. Bamforth, 'Some social and psychological consequences of the long-wall method of coal getting' in *Human Relations*, Spring, 1951, pp. 3–38.
4 *Daily Telegraph*, 29 December 1983, p. 12.
5 I.L. Janus, *Victims of Groupthink*, Harcourt Brace Jovanovich, London, 1972.
6 Institute of Directors, *Guidelines for Directors*, 1982.
7 Mike Woodcock, *Team Development Manual*, second edition, Gower, Aldershot, 1989.
   Dave Francis and Don Young, *Improving Work Groups*, University Associates, San Diego, 1979.
8 Meredith Belbin, *Management Teams: Why They Succeed or Fail*, Heinemann, 1981.

11 Law and order: Justice must prevail

Every community develops a framework of laws which regulate conduct. These provide the ground rules of acceptable behaviour. Organizations exercise considerable power over the lives of employees and their families with managers operating as judge and jury often without a right of appeal. Successful managers devise and honourably administer an appropriate system of rules and regulations. They adopt the value: *justice must prevail*.

Organizations, like all other communities, establish rules of conduct which become codified into systems of laws. Few people doubt the fundamental importance of law in maintaining orderly and productive communities.

Managers act like the government of the country when they develop frameworks for administering justice; in effect the organization is a microcosm of society. Management is, therefore, 'micro-politics in action' and, in the exercise of power, managers become lawmakers and judges.

Managers regularize conduct and dispense justice for two reasons. Firstly, because they are subject to national (or international) legal requirements and, secondly, because they must make laws themselves (codes of conduct, rules and regulations, procedures etc.) to control and co-ordinate their organizations.

In this chapter we concentrate on the second aspect: the manager as lawmaker, judge and jury. Of course, managers should comply, both in letter and spirit (if not always joyfully) with the law of the land.

Managers, often rightly, see interference by politicians as unhelpful. Much behaviour at work is regulated by national laws which limit initiative and add to costs. Employers are no longer free to send children up chimneys or down coal mines! And quite right too.

How much discipline, law and order is desirable within an organization? Many managements emphasize rigid discipline yet some highly successful companies apparently allow a relatively undisciplined environment to flourish. The contribution of law and order to organizations can only be grasped when we understand that some enterprises are inherently different in character from others. The essence of effective management is to choose an approach to lawmaking which provides the correct balance between central regulation and individual initiative.

A simple analysis helps to answer the question. Begin by looking at the work done. Organizations do tasks which are either simple or difficult, routine or innovative. There are four possible permutations:

1   Organizations which perform simple and routine tasks.
2   Organizations which perform difficult and routine tasks.
3   Organizations which perform simple and innovative tasks.
4   Organizations which perform difficult and innovative tasks.

Four distinctly different types of organization are needed to succeed at each permutation of tasks. The role of manager as lawmaker varies in each case. We will examine each organizational type to demonstrate the point.

Simple and routine tasks need a 'production' organization

Simple and routine tasks are typical of production or clerical organizations. Work has to be completed quickly and efficiently. People serve the system and strong discipline is essential. Examples of this type of organization include postal delivery services, hand assembly, food-processing factories and warehouse operations. Managements can predict, almost exactly, what will happen and they establish detailed codes of behaviour to try and ensure that things go exactly as planned. Employees are asked to conform to extensive rules and regulations and they often develop cunning strategies for evading them. In the production organization managers will prescribe as much behaviour as possible yet strive to avoid red tape and meaningless regulations. The

challenge for the organizational lawmaker in the production organization is to control fully what goes on without being labelled a tyrant.

Difficult and routine tasks need a 'professional' organization

Difficult but routine tasks are typical of craft or professional organizations. Work demands specialized knowledge and skill with 'professional' workers taking important decisions. The organization should
be, in some ways, the servant of its specialists. Examples of this type of
organization include hospitals and universities. Managers cannot fully
legislate for the behaviour of specialists as too many complex circumstances occur. Discretion, therefore, passes to the craftsman or professional worker. In 'professional' organizations managers lay down
guidelines for selection of staff, set minimum standards of performance and insist on professional development, regular training and co-
ordination. But detailed or petty regulations will invoke little response;
persuasion is an essential tool. The challenge to the organizational
lawmaker in this form of organization is to set a common direction and
achieve high standards whilst allowing individuals to cherish, develop
and protect their independence.

Simple and innovative tasks need a 'decentralized' organization

Simple but innovative tasks are typical of 'decentralized' organizations
which constantly need to adjust to new situations in their volatile
markets. Consider a business conglomerate. It may have businesses in
aerospace, property, shipping and insurance. Top management cannot
understand each market and must establish management teams to run
each business. Initiative and adaptability at the business team level are
essential.

  The principle is for each division to plan its own strategy. As top
managers cannot predict the specific requirements of each situation
they must develop the sensitivity of those in 'the front line'. Teams must
be created who can become adept at coping with specialized market
conditions . Head office managers should be clear about objectives and
standards and realize that they cannot control all eventualities. They
need to control by setting standards, and by using training and
feedback on performance, which are the appropriate techniques for

regulating behaviour. The challenge to the organizational lawmaker in this form of organization is to establish standards by which performance is judged and enforce these while recognizing that high performance depends on individuals taking initiatives.

Difficult and innovative tasks need an 'organic' organization

Difficult and innovative tasks are typical of research, development and other highly creative functions. New solutions have to be found for 'state of the art' problems and unconventional thinking is often required for a breakthrough. Work is flexible, often in teams but sometimes alone. Examples of this kind of organization are advertising agencies, research laboratories and some hi-tech production units. Management specifies problems to be solved but finds that it cannot set detailed objectives as too little is known about what is possible. Difficult choices, often based on technical debate, must be made and managers take the roles of arbitrators and resource allocators. Unconventional behaviour may be accepted from accomplished individuals. Very successful innovative companies have found that they have to fight against bureaucratic tendencies as these inhibit creativity. Managers in organic organizations insist that regular reporting takes place and a sense of urgency is maintained. However, they avoid rigid systems. The challenge to the organizational lawmaker in this form of organization is to regulate in extremely complex and ever changing situations so that resources are well spent and time is not wasted through the pursuit of self-interest or indecision.

Each of these four organizational types presents particular management challenges. However, each form of organization has unique strengths and is the best choice for certain tasks. Managers should attune their lawmaking style to the needs of the situation. A comprehensive code of discipline is entirely suitable for a production organization, but ludicrously irrelevant to the organic organization. The laws of the organization should, of course, contribute to effectiveness, not increase irrelevant bureaucracy.

The truth, the whole truth and nothing but the truth

Many managers have realized that enterprises thrive best when employees frankly disclose what they think and feel. Without openness, facts are hidden and unhealthy organizational conflicts develop. Openness includes respect for individual opinions and support for the interests of minorities. Openness can be defined as 'clearly conveying facts, arguments and perceptions to those who have influence'.

This definition of openness includes:

- facts (descriptions of what is happening)
- arguments (rational thinking and debate)
- perceptions (emotional values and reactions)
- influence (being heard by people who matter).

All these four elements are linked. Facts bring objectivity, thinking enables arguments to be rational, feeling gives passion, commitment and influence brings potency.

Why should openness deliberately be encouraged by managers? The fundamental reason is that openness is an essential check on the potential abuse of power; especially managerial power. It is readily apparent that few large organizations are true democracies. Those individuals acquiring positions of organizational power are nominees of the existing establishment rather than freely elected representatives of the majority of employees. This makes organizations vulnerable to despotism. Checks and balances are required.

Managers should encourage openness for four reasons: to enhance the quality of decision making, to incorporate minority opinions, to sharpen the conscience of the organization, and to allow frustrations to be vented. We shall examine each reason separately.

We need to enlarge on the research of Professor Irving Janus, summarized in Chapter 10. He alerted managers to the value of openness and the inherent dangers of decision making without full expression of views. He vividly described a management ailment called 'groupthink'.

Janus studied great blunders in decision making and found that top groups often become closed minded and lose touch with reality. They see the world through their own rose-coloured spectacles and resist all attempts to change. He gave an insightful analysis of fiascos in the Cuban Bay of Pigs incident, the North Korean war, Pearl Harbour, the Vietnam War and the Cuban missile crisis, and evolved the following hypothesis:[1]

> The central theme of my analysis can be summarised in the generalization which I offer in the spirit of Parkinson's laws: The more amiability and esprit de corps among the members of a policy making

in-group, the greater is the danger that independent critical thinking will be replaced by groupthink, which is likely to result in irrational and dehumanising actions directed against out groups.

Janus suggests the deliberate encouragement of openness as an antidote to groupthink. He advocates, for example, that 'one or more outside experts or qualified colleagues within the organization who are not core members should be invited to each meeting on a staggered basis and should be encouraged to challenge the views of the core members'.[2]

You will recall that closed groups suffering from groupthink formulate their own interpretation of reality. They do not survey all of the available options; they discard options before examining them for non-obvious gains; they ignore expertise because of the bias of powerful group members, and they give insufficient consideration to the likely reactions of outside groups.

Most management teams are close and cohesive decision-making groups: as such, they are vulnerable to committing such blunders. All too often they develop an isolated approach and become a law unto themselves.

The best antidote to groupthink is openness, which requires evaluating views and proposals after comprehensive debate. Different perspectives, when voiced, shake and test illogical or unrealistic arguments. The quality of decision making largely depends on challenge and debate. Senior groups must take both the decision and the consequences, but they reduce the risk of wrong judgement by seeking diverse viewpoints as part of their information collection process. Insecure and blinkered managers fear to solicit views and take counsel, and they lose the capability to take wise decisions because of their narrow-mindedness; they readily become victims of groupthink.

Who makes the laws?

Many organizations have the complication of two lawmaking bodies in their midst. In addition to the formal management structure there is an alternative trade union system which also makes rules and has ways of achieving compliance. When these two power groups clash (as they often do) enormous effort is needed to seek common ground. Almost all managers are committed to management-led organizations and, therefore, see strong alternative power groups as a threat. The solution is easy to advise but difficult to practise: management should maintain its power by demonstrating its supremacy through skills competence and principled good practice.

This requires the adoption of an approach to lawmaking appropriate to local needs. A management style effective in Mansfield, England, may become ineffective when applied in Bombay or San Diego. To some extent regional differences can be observed within a country. In Britain, for example, a factory in Plymouth can have a very different character from one manufacturing similar products in Liverpool. Informal conventions shape behaviour, like a giant invisible puppet master pulling strings in the organization to give it a distinctive character.

The study of the manager as lawmaker requires exploration of a further dimension: culture. Organizational culture influences individuals and managers are well advised to try to build a culture which facilitates high performance. When opportunities occur to mould culture, they are well worth seizing. Although the task of the organization is more important than culture in determining the kinds of laws needed, 'culture' influences how laws are applied and how justice is dispensed.

We have argued that managers need to create relevant frameworks of law and order in organizations by first looking at the tasks undertaken. Managers are advised to study carefully their actual situation and devise appropriate strategies. The twelve questions below can help in directing attention to those areas important for the organizational lawmaker.

1   What size is the organization?
2   What work is done?
3   How difficult are the tasks?
4   How much innovation is required?
5   What regulations should continue unchanged?
6   What regulations are decreasing performance and should be reduced or eliminated?
7   What new disciplines are likely to add to effectiveness?
8   How does the local community culture influence behaviour?
9   How effectively could new regulations be enforced?
10   What historical factors limit freedom of action?
11   How strong are pressure groups which can resist management policy?
12   What are the key success factors of your industry?

Codes of conduct

At the most basic level, managers devise legal systems which regulate behaviour in these areas:

- attendance (hours, punctuality etc.)
- honesty (theft, sabotage etc.)
- conflict (physical violence etc.)
- discipline (who's in charge of what)
- health and safety (legal and organizational requirements)
- basic standards (hygiene etc.)
- commercial secrecy (what not to tell whom)
- procedures for administering justice (including the involvement of appropriate trades unions etc.)
- punishments (type and appeal procedure)
- rewards (remuneration, promotion, perks).

Organizations need legal systems to spell out codes of behaviour and enforce them. Such prescriptions should be just, clear, relevant and, most importantly, enforceable. Where unfair, obsolete or unenforceable regulations exist they undermine the integrity of the whole system.

Managers also act in the role of judge. In fact, they often combine the roles of lawmaker, judge and jury even though, in almost all communities, particularly democratic ones, it has been decided that the legislature and the judiciary should be separate. Most national legal systems even split the two roles of the judge: determining guilt and passing sentence. But many managers play all of these roles.

Many would argue that management's power to act as lawmaker, judge and jury is inherently unfair on those who are managed. It certainly places a great responsibility on managers who must strive hard to administer justice fairly. There are few checks and balances built in to many organizations' legal systems. To add further complexity the word 'justice' describes a moving target. Justice requires fair, administration of prevailing laws.

It is useful to reflect on what fairness means. Of necessity it must be 'in accord with a sense of natural justice'. Schoolchildren talking of respected teachers describe them as 'firm but fair'. Fairness is a quality much admired when present and its absence is despised. Managers increase the chances of fair judgement by adopting five principles:

1   Careful selection of those who act as judges.
2   Placing an emphasis on collecting objective evidence.

3 Having clear and explicit procedures.
4 Giving the opportunity for the 'accused' to fully state his/her case.
5 Ensuring that there is a right of appeal.

Rewards change behaviour and learning is reinforced by repetition. Conversely, behaviour which is unrewarded tends to be reduced or eliminated. Behaviour Modification has been proven a valid theory with animals as well as man. For example, in one case experimenters were able, by using suitable rewards, to cause a mouse to blush in one ear only. When regulations or 'laws' in human communities are examined, the following insights emerge:

- appropriate behaviour should be rewarded
- repetition is usually necessary
- feedback must happen quickly
- inappropriate behaviour must not be rewarded
- punishment may aid 'unlearning'.

These principles are useful to managers as they emphasize the positive use of systems of justice. Punishment is available, but only as a last resort. Most effort should be devoted to finding rapid ways of rewarding positive behaviour. An organizational legal framework based on these principles will achieve positive motivation. Managements should not regulate by suppression and coercion. The acceptance of regulation and order is based on people recognizing the benefits of an organized life.

The costs of breaches in the rule of law can be severe. Employees in a food factory are informally permitted to wear their hair uncovered and a girl is severely injured when her long hair is caught in machinery. A director uses company funds for currency speculation and millions are lost. Poor timekeeping and sloppy standards are tolerated in a vehicle assembly plant with production efficiencies below similar plants on the continent and eventually the factory is closed. No-one gains and the derisory remarks about petty regulations sound hollow when 'the chickens come home to roost'.

Recently, we have seen many organizations rediscover the importance of regulations, partly inspired by American and Japanese management techniques. A good illustration is the fast food business. For many years down-at-heel fast food outlets were pre-eminent; then came MacDonalds! The success of the MacDonalds formula was like a cold shower to the opposition. MacDonalds consistently maintained high standards and attracted more and more customers. There were two secrets: firstly, its business concept was sound and, secondly, MacDonalds is highly structured and disciplined; a well regulated example of the production organization described earlier in this chapter. Competitors, if they were to survive, had to revise their company approach to law and order and set new standards of performance and customer care.

The lessons of this chapter are fundamental. Successful organizations are open, fair and orderly societies with appropriate legal systems. Managers must use their judicial powers wisely and constructively.

Summary

Core principles

- all organizations need legal systems
- managers must make laws, and administer justice
- managers should work within the law of the land, but seek to influence national lawmakers to enact helpful legislation
- organizational laws should be 'fit for their purposes'
- 'production' organizations must be very carefully controlled
- 'professional' organizations must maintain high standards of selection and training
- 'decentralized' organizations must be allowed to go their own way if the results are adequate
- 'organic' organizations must fight bureaucracy and encourage teamwork
- managers should review the special character of their own organization prior to making laws
- corporate legal systems should lay down basic codes of conduct
- managers should be aware that they act as judge and jury and few checks and balances exist in most organizations to ensure that justice is done
- organizational laws are best used to provide positive motivation.

Five steps to ensure that justice prevails

1   Ask each manager to:
    (a) list those regulations which are kept
    (b) list those regulations which are ignored

    (c) list those regulations which appear irrelevant

    (d) list any new regulations considered desirable.

Use the information to produce a detailed report for the top management team, as a prelude to a review of regulations in your organization.

2   Invite a practising barrister specializing in industrial law to visit you and

    (a) assess how far your present practices conform to legal requirements

    (b) comment on justice in your organization, in particular how your approach would stand up if it was on trial.

3   Arrange for an organizational consultant or researcher to conduct a one-day seminar for top management on how organizations control and regulate themselves. Try to obtain an insight into how organizations vary according to tasks performed (contingency theory). Use the information to analyze your own organization and determine whether your internal legal system should be altered in principle or application.

4   Examine your present internal regulations and codes of conduct to determine whether they are expressed positively or negatively. Use the skills of your marketing department to devise a revised guide which is comprehensive, comprehensible and positive.

5   Look afresh at procedures for dispensing discipline to try to achieve swifter feedback, so that the punishment follows soon after the crime. Devise criteria for judging success, and a means of monitoring performance.

References

1   I.L. Janus, *Victims of Groupthink*, Harcourt Brace Jovanovich, London, 1972, p. 13.

2   Ibid., p. 214.

Part V

MANAGING THE ENVIRONMENT

12 Defence: Know thine enemy

For many organizations It Is a dog-eat-dog world. In every commercial organization talented people are planning how to increase their
business at the expense of the competition. Non-commercial organizations are often under threat from those who provide the funds.
Successful managers study external threats and formulate a strong
defence. They adopt the value: *know thine enemy*.

Every living organism can be threatened and organizations are no
exception. There are enemies without and within. It is imperative to
recognize the world as a dangerous place and study the enemy.
    In this chapter we debate three questions:

    Why a warlike approach to management?
    Who are the enemy without?
    Who are the enemy within?

Why a warlike approach to management?

It is easy to underestimate the importance of military thinking to
strategic planning. Consider an example. One of the reasons for the
success of Japanese business in the postwar period has been identified
as the 'Samurai' factor.[1]
    The time-honoured samurai principles are:

- know the opposition
- live harmoniously

- master all weapons
- concentrate your resources
- respect uncertainty
- if you cannot win, form an alliance
- fight at a time of your own choosing
- seize and retain the initiative
- balance strategy with detail.

Many Japanese leaders owe much to the Samurai tradition. They see their activities as a benign form of warfare. In order to understand how such warlike values provide a competitive edge it is necessary to examine the principles of good generalship.

A classic analysis made by General Von Clausewitz[2] identified the nine principles of successful warfare.

Principle One: Every operation should be directed towards a clearly defined, decisive and attainable objective

Although this principle reads like a motherhood statement there are many cases where it has been ignored. Another military historian, Colonel Summers[3] describes the results of a research study which showed that 'almost 70 per cent of the Army Generals who managed the [Vietnam] war were uncertain as to its objective. [This demonstrated] a deep seated strategic failure: the inability of policy makers to frame tangible, obtainable goals.'

There have been many cases where non-military organizations have suffered the same fate: Jaguar cars in the 1970s and Midland Bank's takeover of the Crocker Bank are two examples.

Principle Two: Seize, retain and exploit the initiative

A strong defence will deter and protect, but it will not win a war. An offensive initiative is needed, although a direct frontal assault rarely leads to victory.

There are five ways to seize the initiative:

1 Frontal attack – an assault against the enemy's main source of strength.
2 Flank attack – an attempt to bypass the main lines of defence.
3 Guerilla attack – an assault from behind.

4   Penetration – an attack from within.
5   Self-attack – an attack against your own capability in order to confront your weaknesses and bring about self-improvement.

Principle Three: Concentrate combat power at the decisive place and time

There are always some decisive moments when one side gains long-term advantage. An aim of strategic thinking is to see the potential of a decisive victory before it occurs and amass forces to win that battle.

There have been many cases where organizations have been overwhelmed by the size, ferocity or skill of the opposition. The chief skill needed by the management is to deploy your resources at the point of your competitor's weakness – the art of positioning.

Principle Four: Allocate minimum combat power to the secondary efforts

It is impossible to be strong everywhere, and so it is necessary to deploy forces in sufficient concentrations to make a decisive difference.

This principle is often ignored by growing businesses who take on too much and spread themselves too thinly. Over-ambition is a common fault. Hence weakness and inadequate resources are devoted to the primary objectives. Even large companies can become over-extended. For example, the Japanese earth-moving equipment company, Komatsu, had much success until it tried to defeat Caterpillar on its own ground in the USA. It is vital to determine the scope of operations, and not become over-stretched.

Principle Five: Place the enemy at a position of disadvantage through the flexible use of your combat power

Once a strategy becomes static it provides opponents with the time to prepare their attack. Constant change gives an edge, since it takes time for the enemy to detect what you are doing.

Organizations must get used to constant re-organizing and developing new ways of addressing old problems. Creativity is always required.

They need to determine their competitive edge (whether it is price, quality or service) and work at maintaining real advantage.

Principle Six: For every objective there should be a unity of command under one responsible commander

Confusion about who is in charge has led to many blunders, both military and commercial. There is no doubt that one of the most effective ways to co-ordinate effort is to make one person responsible: the integration then takes place in one person's brain.

The principle draws attention to the need for a responsible commander. The centralization of decision-making authority in one man or woman has inherent risks. It is vital that such people should be an elite.

Also the principle causes us to question the use of matrix and consensus management techniques, as these spread responsibility and can cause confusion and evasion.

Principle Seven: Never permit the enemy to acquire an unexpected advantage

It is imperative to assess your competition constantly and predict all of the hostile actions that they might be capable of undertaking. The story of the Trojan Horse has been repeated in many contexts since 1184 BC.

It is essential to have an intimate knowledge of your industry and its competitive environment. Early warning signs of an enemy offensive can often be detected, despite your opponents' best efforts to disguise their intent. All too often the challenges of the moment cause managers to wear blinkers and ignore the threats until it is too late.

Principle Eight: Strike the enemy at a time, place, and in a manner for which he is unprepared

It is difficult to surprise opponents at the strategic level, but often tactical advantage can be gained. This requires a conscious effort to keep the opposition unsure of your true objectives. By spreading confusion you gain more opportunity to surprise.

Speed is also needed. Rapid change is, in essence, confusing to those who are not party to your plan. The faster you move the more likely it is that you can strike unexpectedly.

Principle Nine: Keep all plans simple, because even the simplest is difficult to execute

A simple plan is needed because many people must take initiatives to turn the plan into a reality. Complex plans are difficult to interpret and so people make invalid interpretations and effort is dissipated.

Plans have to be implemented in less than ideal circumstances. Sustaining effort is always a problem. Simple plans enable individual efforts to be focused and supervision exercised.

Who are the enemy without?

All organizations have competitors or potential competitors. A competitor is 'an organization that is perceived by customers as providing an equivalent good/service to your organization and which meets a similar need or want'.

In order to study the competition it is necessary to organize an intelligence operation. This requires:

- a 'war room' where all competitor information is stored and displayed
- a task force which contains senior line managers, an excellent business analyst and some foot soldiers
- speed – don't allow the intelligence task force to become bureaucratic
- strict standards of objectivity
- a list of actual competitors
- a list of potential competitors
- a file on each competitor containing:
    - their annual reports and accounts for last few years
    - relevant press cuttings on their company
    - any specialized consultancy studies available
    - details of patents and potential new patents
- a file on your industry containing:
    - statistics on the market and its growth (historical and projected)
    - specialized written assessments of the market
- a list of the 'bad' competitors (i.e. those who could and might seriously damage your business) – develop a detailed file on each
- a detailed history of each competitor
- an assessment of the dangers that you are being technologically leapfrogged

- a study of your 'bad' competitors' management team detailing:
  who has the power?
  what is his/her history?
  what are their top team strengths and weaknesses?

It is vital to involve the top team in ensuring that the research data is relevant. Brief reports for top team intelligence briefings should be prepared. The key data should be presented in easy-to-visualize charts, tables, graphs, cartoons etc. The process should be repeated often.

Not all threats are negative. Even though fair competition is a form of attack, this external challenge, when ethical, is a force which sharpens and stimulates.

Who are the enemy within?

Internal threats are usually destructive, as they undermine the integrity of the organization. Like woodworm in the timbers of an old building, organizational civil war often has catastrophic results.

There are seven potential threats to the internal integrity of organizations.

1   Lack of focus so that the organization loses its way.
2   Inadequate management development so that resources are wasted (see Chapter 4).
3   Poor integration between functions so that co-ordination is weak (see Chapter 7).
4   Low commercial awareness so that survival is threatened (see Chapter 8).
5   Slow innovation so that the organization becomes obsolete (see Chapter 13).
6   Lack of consensus so that the objectives of the organization are not shared by all employees and people do not care about the success of the organization (see Chapters 9 and 10).
7   Structured attacks from alternative power groups so that management's freedom is impaired.

We shall examine here the first and the last of these threats.

Lack of focus so that the organization loses its way

Lack of focus is a familiar managerial problem. In our consulting practice we are often asked to help top management teams in their search for a clear and viable identity. We find that it is vital for each unit to identify its Strategic Driving Force.[4] There are twelve possibilities.

Strategic Driving Force One: state-of-the-art   This organization is a leader in its chosen field. The state-of-the-art organization generates business by doing things in more advanced or cleverer ways than anyone else. It is a powerhouse of creativity and is constantly changing as new technology develops. Customers are attracted by getting the best or newest goods or services.

Strategic Driving Force Two: professional service   This organization provides its customers with highly skilled individual services. The professional service organization enables qualified individuals to carry out their specialized tasks. Customers are attracted because they have complex human needs which can be met.

Strategic Driving Force Three: product producer   This organization produces goods or services and offers them to defined markets. The product producer organization has product ranges which are not tailor-made for individual customers. Customers are attracted by products which are desirable and good value for money.

Strategic Driving Force Four: experience provider   This organization provides people with experiences which they enjoy or value. The experience provider organization generates business by meeting a human need for sensation, stimulation or edification. It aims to understand totally and fulfil a need or want. This may be for entertainment (in a theatre), for excitement (on an action holiday), for fantasy (in a strip club), for interest (in a museum), for spiritual experience (in a church) or any human needs. Such an organization concentrates on the depth and breadth of the receiver's experience.

Strategic Driving Force Five: market server   This organization fulfils all the needs of a defined market. There are many markets and market segments like fishermen, electrical contractors, stamp collectors, secretaries and so on. Customers are attracted to the organization because it can meet most or all of their needs.

Strategic Driving Force Six: system provider   This organization

enables other organizations to communicate or co-ordinate. It generates business by enabling complex operations to be performed. Such
systems may be electronic, logistical or managerial; the essence is
providing a capability to others which enables them to manage complexity.

Strategic Driving Force Seven: production contractor   The production contractor organization provides a facility for others to get things
built, constructed, repaired, adapted or manufactured. It generates
business by enabling specialist tasks to be done for those without the
will or resources to do the work themselves. The essence of its business
is that it contracts to supply specific services which maintain or add
value to products.

Strategic Driving Force Eight: profit cow   This organization makes
money for its owners. It is solely a resource for making profit and is
exploited only so long as it is the best way of using the capital tied up in
ownership. All managerial decisions are taken with the intention of
maximizing profitability. It generates business by providing channels to
exploit the commercial acumen of its owners.

Strategic Driving Force Nine: resource ownership   This organization
acquires valuable resources and exploits them. There are two types of
resource ownership enterprises. The first owns land, space, minerals,
raw materials, crops, animals, or things cultivated and grown. This
type generates business because it possesses and distributes commodi-
ties which others need and want. The second type is the large conglomerate which acquires a portfolio of companies which are measured on
their performance. The portfolio is treated as an estate and adapted to
maximize profitability over the medium and long term.

Strategic Driving Force Ten: distribution capability   This organization moves physical products to where they are needed – by air, rail, sea,
road, canal, space flight, mail etc. It generates business by providing
systems and vehicles for efficient transportation of tangible items
without damaging them. It exploits its distribution capability in as
many ways as possible.

Strategic Driving Force Eleven: maintenance of order   This organization maintains order. It protects property and services, people, peace,

and the rights of the citizen. It generates business by enabling other activities to proceed unhindered. There are two types of maintenance of order organizations. The first is concerned with security. On the national scale the armed forces have this role; local police, courts, security guards etc. perform similar functions at the community level. The second type provides services like cleaning, repairing, painting, maintaining, monitoring, inspecting and surveying.

Strategic Driving Force Twelve: self-expression   This organization provides facilities for members to do what they need or want to do. Satisfaction includes enjoyment, self-expression, enlightenment, comradeship, support, stimulation etc. The organization sustains itself because people wish to contribute and give voluntarily. Such organizations are frequently non-commercial.

These twelve strategic driving forces provide the basis of a viable 'compelling vision' which becomes the single driving force of the organization. The viability of the choice is partly determined by the environment – that is why the analysis of enemies is vital. Once determined, *all* aspects of the organization should be shaped to actualize the driving force.

Structured attacks from alternative power groups so that management's freedom is impaired

The seventh threat has been particularly important in recent years and it largely concerns the role of trade unions. These institutions have repeatedly demonstrated that they can undermine the managerial power base. But the picture is patchy; some managers have struck constructive bargains with trade unions and others admit a grudging respect for their single-mindedness. The extent to which managers are affected by union activities varies greatly.

The stance of trade unions should not be taken lightly. There is no doubt that many have a distinguished record. Anyone examining their history over the past century will recognize the honourable battles that have been fought against managerial injustice.

Exploitation was practised in the past by bosses. The image of young children working down coalmines is sufficient to make the point. Organized protest proved the only effective way to counter such abuses.

The fact that trade unions developed in every industrial country demonstrates the universality of the need for them.

In many countries unions have gained strength by differentiating themselves from employers. As such they may be accused of promoting – sometimes explicitly, sometimes insidiously – class warfare. They require periodic conflict to give them a sustained raison d'être. So trade unions seek opportunities to contest the management and often define their role as 'winning battles'. The interdependence of much industry gives unions enormous power to disrupt.

Let us examine the threat in more detail. At first glance trade unions appear to be fighting for the downtrodden, yet, ironically, their struggles may often have had the opposite effect. Nobel prize-winning economist Friedrich Hayek, writing about the UK economy, stated:[5]

> As long as the general opinion makes it politically impossible to deprive the Trades Unions of their coercive powers, an economic recovery in Great Britain is also impossible . . . It is an illusion that the problem Britain now faces can be solved by negotiation with the present Trades Union leaders. They owe their power precisely to the scope for abusing the privileges which the law has granted them. It is the rank and file of the workers, including many Trades Union members who ultimately suffer from this abuse.

Although the abuse of trade union power has been the biggest potential inner threat over the past fifty years there are many other hazards which erode management power. There has been a decline in the acceptance of the legitimacy of authority in society. Attitudes towards the police, urban riots, and sports ground hooliganism are all symptoms of this fundamental change in social attitudes.

Management's power base requires a sense of unity. The only sound basis for any organization is a group of people pulling together for a common end. It is disastrous for an organization to lose sight of customers' needs and waste energy in ponderous internal debate. The flabbiness which results from such 'civil war' struggles costs many organizations dearly.

On balance, attack is the best form of defence. If managers are humane and professional they counter all of the seven threats listed at the beginning of this chapter. This is only achievable if management takes a responsible stance towards its workforce. For example, trade union strength comes partly from the inadequacy and unprofessionalism of management. An unprincipled organization deserves to be constantly harassed by threats, but a well managed organization does not.

We have seen many companies win by changing their posture and redefining the conventional 'contract' between the company and the workforce. This provides a crucial foundation for an integrated organization. For example, the Nissan company made it quite clear that it would build a car plant in England only if it negotiated a satisfactory agreement with a single union which eliminated demarcation and discouraged disruptive conflicts.

John Harvey-Jones, ex-Chairman of ICI, puts it this way: 'The reality of the future is that the interests of trade unions, union membership and management lie together and it is the responsibility of management to take the lead in making this collaboration more effective and more creative.'[6]

Where the internal battles have been won there are great benefits. The start up of the new 'sinter' steelmaking plant at Redcar was delayed in 1978 by the Boilermakers Union who refused to operate with new manning levels and working practices. Yet with agreement there is now full flexibility among the 40-strong workforce, down by 20 since commissioning. Operators have replaced tradesmen's mates on maintenance tasks. Craftsmen work across craft boundaries. Through excellent management, comprehensive training and a co-operative workforce the plant holds the world's sinter output record. It operates at almost 100 per cent efficiency, product quality is unrivalled and energy use is better than Japanese or European standards.[7]

There are some interesting initiatives in seeking common ground between employees and managers. One particularly valuable effort was put together by The Industrial Society who produced a declaration from twelve industrialists and trade union leaders. The principles make interesting reading, and argue that the best form of defence is not to go to war in the first place. The key points include:

- management should recognize employees' right to belong to an independent trade union, recognize a representative trade union for negotiating purposes and encourage employees to belong to a trade union when recognized
- trade unions should recognize the responsibility of management to concern itself with the interests of all employees, seek to resolve inter-union disputes, reflect the views of their members, seeking to involve all of them through effective procedures

- management should consult trade unions before deciding upon changes which affect their members, enable employees to participate in the formulation of relevant management policies
- trade unions should accept the challenge of proper consultation and share the responsibility for developing the correct policies for change, by making suggestions and using the knowledge of their members to make the operation successful
- management should be efficient, inventive, and ingenious in expanding the scope for real jobs
- trade unions should give commitment to the success of the enterprise and work for the creation of more jobs.

The Industrial Society's document argues that the proper relationship between management and other employees is a bargain based on an acceptance of the importance of commercial viability. We agree; the best form of defence is to make the thought of war impossible. Management must manage and resist potential threats to its power. This is an aggressive stance which, the authors believe, can only be justified when management does its job well and adopts high principles.

We began this chapter by looking at how to win battles. We will end by looking at the guidelines for protection. There are ten strategies for defence which have proven their worth since the Trojan Wars. The ingredients of successful defence are:

- awareness of threat so that we are always watchful
- a good system for gathering intelligence so that we know our enemy
- constant training so that we are ready for the enemy
- predicting the likely nature of an attack so that we can be ready
- contingency planning so that we can swing into action without delay
- using our imagination so that we can outwit the enemy
- keeping our defensive equipment up-to-date so that we are not outgunned
- engendering pride so that people feel that they have something for which to fight
- giving emotional support to 'the troops' so that their morale remains high
- having high-quality generals so that people are well led.

These rules of defence are directly applicable within organizations, but there is a danger. In adopting an aggressively defensive stance the manager may well provoke the feared behaviour. Belligerence for its own sake is counterproductive. However, there is no excuse for inaction; enemies must be identified and fought.

Summary

Core principles

- Managers should be wary of threat from within and without
- clarity of objectives is essential
- strive to retain the initiative
- concentrate your resources
- retain flexibility and the capacity to surprise
- ensure that the command structure is 100 per cent clear
- predict the threats from your potential enemies
- keep plans simple: do not confuse yourself
- fair competition is a positive threat (it sharpens you)
- internal threats are usually destructive
- lack of focus is a major threat; the top team must determine the strategic driving force of the organization
- structured opposition, particularly from trade unions, has been a serious internal threat; management must reduce dissent and eliminate the reasons for trade union power
- finding common ground (as in the Industrial Society Declaration) is helpful
- a strong defence is always necessary.

Five steps towards knowing thine enemy

1 Arrange for a military historian to give a presentation to your top team. Ensure that the principles of military successes are well explained. Examine your strategy and tactics to see whether you are lacking. Try to find practical ways to implement the proven principles.
2 Consider the twelve strategic driving forces described in this chapter and choose the one that is right for your organization. Include the definition in your mission statement, and require all senior functional managers to report on how they are going to adapt their department's performance to assist in the enhancement of the chosen strategic driving force.

3 Create a top management study group to assess what benefits the organization and its employees gain from trade unions. Learn the personal philosophies of relevant trade union officials and elected representatives. Try to determine the level of threat which each offers. Develop alternative routes for people to express their opinions (e.g. attitude surveys) so that the power base of unions is weakened. Ensure they know that their views are heard. Act on the basis of your views about how industrial relations should be managed.

4 Give your personnel professionals the best possible training in negotiation skills. Ask them to visit those organizations with a good record of defence against internal threats. Use intensive training to improve their skills.

5 List organizations who have achieved a good relationship with their trade unions. Visit them to find out how they did it. See how many of the lessons can be employed in your own organization. Carefully review what benefits are gained by employees and seek to offer these by management initiative.

References

1 See review of Joseph Rudzinski and Harutoshi Mayuzami, *The Samurai Factor*, in *The Work Research Unit Bulletin*, London, Spring 1987, p. 8.
2 General Von Clausewitz, *On War*, Penguin Books, Harmondsworth, 1968.
3 Colonel H.G. Summers, *On Strategy*, Presidio Press, Novato, 1982.
4 For an extended discussion of this concept see Dave Francis, *Unblocking Organizational Communication*, Gower, Aldershot, 1987.
5 Friedrich Hayek, *1980s Unemployment and the Unions*, Institute of Economic Affairs, London, 1980.
6 *Personnel Management*, May 1984, p. 41.
7 *Lloyds Bank Review*, no. 152, pp. 21–2.

13 Competitiveness: Survival of the fittest

The capacity to be competitive is the only sure-fire recipe for survival. Usually this truth is readily understood at the top level, but it is far harder for the message to be appreciated throughout the organization. Successful managers take all necessary steps to be competitive. They know that in the world of commerce it is the best who survive, and the weakest who go to the wall. They adopt the value: *survival of the fittest*.

In 1984 the Chinese Communist Party announced radical changes in their philosophy of industrial development. A thirty-nine-page document, describing a new structure for industry, stated that productive organizations would be expected to make profits and pay taxes. The State will 'force businesses to compete so that only the best survive'. These radical proposals, said to have been devised by China's elder statesman, Deng Xiaoping, were designed to redress the lack of vitality in industry. The document states that 'enthusiasm, initiative and creativity of the urban enterprises for production and operations, as well as 80 million workers and staff members, must be brought into full play'. Mike Woodcock spent two weeks in China and visited many organizations. He saw a close parallel between Deng Xiaoping's reforms and some of the broad principles of nineteenth-century enterprise. China appears to have discovered the basic truth that competition encourages people to excel. As Mike remarked 'Many of the Chinese I met may call themselves Communists, but to me they were rapidly becoming Capitalists in overalls'.

Human beings compete with each other in most situations. The 'survival of the fittest' principle runs deep. Teenage boys in the African Kau tribe spend hours weaving their hair into fantastic designs, helped by ample quantities of dung, in their eager quest to be considered the most handsome in the group. Greek athletes developed the Olympic Games to test physical prowess and the widows of Florida vie with each other to travel to the world's most interesting places. Everywhere competition brings out the latent potential in people. A runner uses the services of a pacer to push him through the first part of the race, then competes with the clock for the final impetus. Reluctant joggers know it is difficult to puff and pant around their course alone; it is easier to take exercise playing a close game of squash. Although human nature is extremely adaptable, competitiveness is such a pervasive force that, for all practical purposes, it can be called a human instinct.

Competition is a trigger for the release of human energy and can be deliberately used, by managers, in the pursuit of excellence. In our opinion managers know too little about the positive merits of competition. Essentially, competition is a way of organizing human affairs which clearly demonstrates who wins, and provides a motivating factor which, perhaps more than any other, has led to outstanding achievement.

Competitiveness is frequently derided as a symptom of a juvenile mentality. For example, some schools are preventing children from entering athletic competitions because, it is alleged, they encourage elitism. Yet most people enjoy coming into contact with excellence. They applauded *Chariots of Fire*, a film which explored the depths of the competitive urge. In it the athletes competed with other runners, their social environment, and most powerfully, with themselves. The result was a beautiful and moving portrait of a superb human achievement – which emerged through competition.

However, like all powerful tools, competition, when used in the wrong way, rapidly becomes counter-productive. Excessive competition provokes groups who should work together to become sworn enemies and individuals attempt to outdo each other instead of collaborating. Destructive competition must be identified and fought. The essence of using the energizing force of competition is 'know your real opponent'.

'Winning' is a learnable competence. People will often admit that they lack assertion, drive and a winner mentality. This may be traced to a lack of development in personal competitiveness. It can be argued persuasively that, over the past decades, advisers to management have placed too much emphasis on collaboration and harmonization and have tended, wrongly, to see consensus as the superior way of achieving the best.

A worthy opponent should be greatly valued. The story is told in Westminster about a new Member of Parliament who referred to the opposition parties as 'the enemy'. He was soon told by an experienced back bencher: 'Always remember, the opposition are your opponents, not your enemy. They sharpen your wits. Your enemies are on this side of the house because they are the people who would personally benefit from your downfall'.

Competition can be a creative and motivating force in the workplace, but when it is the sole principle guiding behaviour it undermines the quality of life. Someone who relentlessly competes for the sole purpose of self aggrandizement may gain material riches but is driven by obsession and often finds financial achievements hollow. Competition is an essential ingredient for a productive managerial philosophy but it must be enriched by a desire to enhance the quality of life.

The British Institute of Directors say:[1]

The free enterprise system depends fundamentally on the ability of individuals to choose to spend their money on the products of one business rather than those of another. Nothing is more calculated to bring free enterprise into disrepute than attempts to secure unfair advantage over customers, whether by failure to disclose information relevant to the customer's choice, by attempts to set aside statutory safeguards, for customers, or by an unwillingness to take adequate account of, or provide adequate compensation for, possible damages to health implicit in a particular product. The customer is the businessman's friend, not his enemy.

Competition in organizations

Within organizations competition should be focused on raising standards, maintaining a high level of achievement and motivation. We will examine competition at five levels:

1   Individual versus individual.
2   Team versus team.
3   Unit versus unit.
4   Organization versus organization.

5   International competition.

The competitive principle is a two-edged sword. When used unhelpfully it results in waste, backbiting, secrecy and interpersonal criticism. Organizational performance decreases when those who should co-operate adopt a competitive stance. This does not mean that the principle of competition should be abandoned: rather, it must be used selectively and judiciously.

Individual versus individual

Competition is first encountered in the recruitment of new people. The quality of human resource is crucial to effectiveness, so it is imperative that the best people are chosen. It is worth making great effort to facilitate genuine competition between job applicants. Choice at the recruitment stage is one of management's most valued devices for maintaining control.

People are different and should be treated as such. Selection is common to all species. Charles Darwin studied the turtles of the Galapagos Islands to discover the principles of evolution, but he could also have looked at successful organizations and found ample evidence to support his views. The successful concept is simple: the fittest are the ones who thrive. The successful manager seeks to select the fittest.

Within the organization competition between individuals can be a truly valuable motivator, but it must be handled carefully to prevent losers from giving up, becoming resentful and failing to 'play the game'. Success should be something to which all can aspire, and continued successes are necessary to sustain motivation.

The first focus of competition is within the individual. This can be encouraged by the most enduring management technique, Management by Objectives, which has been with us for more than twenty-five years. Although the concept can be over-elaborated the essential points are valuable: boss and subordinate agree measurable targets which become psychological contracts. Management by Objectives uses the basic form of the competitive principle: people are provided with the means to compete against agreed performance levels.

In some jobs it is possible to use competition between individuals as a primary motivating force. Many salesmen and women leave their homes early in the morning and bounce into their potential customers' premises full of joviality and positiveness. They are partly motivated by relentless competition with other sales staff. They may not want to be at the top of the tree but they have to compete simply to keep their jobs. One salesman put it this way: 'I spend my life being measured and I know my place in the pecking order all the time. It's the thing that drives me on!'

Team versus team

Competition between teams can also be used to advantage. Next time you go into a MacDonald's restaurant (and wherever you live in the world there is likely to be one not too far away) look at the name badges of the staff. Some have stars where others have blank spaces. Each star represents a tested level of competence in a particular aspect of the operation of the branch. One star is gained for counter service, another for preparing french fries and so on. Although it is individuals who have to achieve set standards, the motivational power of the implied competition between teams is considerable. The morning shift is inspired to achieve higher standards than the afternoon shift, the french friers than the counter staff etc. This leads not only to higher standards but also to faster learning as team members urge their colleagues to qualify and thus raise the competence and standing of the team.

For many workers the competitive principle may seem irrelevant. One job is interwoven with another and individual achievement is difficult to identify. However, it is often possible to use the second level of competition, the work team, as the unit of comparison. Teams can often be encouraged to strive to demonstrate their superior potency and competence.

The following questions may help you to decide whether inter-team competition is a relevant motivational technique for you:

* Do the teams have similar objectives?
* Could there be objective measures of performance?
* Are few areas of collaboration needed?
* Can rewards be given for success?
* Are all teams likely to be 'turned on' by competition?
* Can feedback on relative success be given quickly?

If the answer to these questions is 'yes' then the teams are likely to benefit from inter-team competition. This approach demands:

* a 'fair' comparison

- rapid exchange of performance data
- the chance for all teams to win and fail
- prizes for success (recognition is often enough)
- leadership which helps turn the experience of failure into a desire to win next time.

Unit versus unit

The third level of competition may sometimes be useful: organizational units can compete with each other. Chains of retail stores often set comparative targets for shop performance which are regularly shared and prizes given to the successful. Some of the motivational techniques may seem juvenile. For example, one large electrical retailer rewards oustanding stores by a visit from a coachload of men dressed in weird animal skins. These creatures enter the shop with much razzmatazz, cavort with the staff and present prizes. Ridiculous, of course, but people enjoy it and it helps energize their working lives.

Large organizations frequently structure themselves into units or divisions, each devoted to a particular market. Direct competition is difficult because units have unique problems and opportunities. However, progressive accountants can provide techniques for statistical comparison, such as:

- capital employed
- return on assets employed
- gross profit
- net profit
- growth trends
- market shares
- output per employee
- cost comparison with competitors
- investment in research and development
- level of complaints
- added value per employee.

Such comparative data, when carefully analyzed, enable apparently dissimilar units to be compared for competitive purposes and provide an essential basis for decision making and communication. Few accountants would volunteer that their most important task is to exploit the competitive urge, but we see this role as one of their most important contributions.

Successful organizations have found ways to 'institutionalize' competition. Dave Francis consults with a vigorous British electronics company which needed continuous innovation in order to survive. Their technical development programme was controlled by a complex procedure but top management became aware that its rational planning system was filtering out 'rogue' ideas and opportunistic chances. It realized that this was not good enough. A parallel system was instituted to encourage 'product champions'. Any individual could propose new product ideas and a competition was held. The company gave three months sabbatical to allow the winning idea to be explored. At all times at least one person in the company was on sabbatical. The resultant flow of creativity was of great value.

Your organization versus the rest

The fourth level of competition is almost always desirable: competition between organizations. One paper bag manufacturer competes with another; as a result both are sharpened and kept dynamic. Without competition neither has the strong incentive to change or critically re-examine existing practices.

Organizations must compete to meet the real needs of the customer. The former chairman of Unilever, Sir David Orr, said: 'I always want to keep a close eye on the customer. If the business is not continually adjusting to what the customer requires, then trouble is probably just around the corner.'

There is always the risk that another organization will make your product or supply your service better or cheaper than you can. This threat should keep everyone on their toes, but there is another interesting side effect: organizations strive to be different from their competitors by finding and maintaining a sustainable competitive advantage. In this way innovation is encouraged and creativity valued. Lord Murray, retired General Secretary of the British TUC, said: 'Industry has to deliver the right goods in the right quantity and of the right quality at the right time'. It is ironic that the entrenched and protected viewpoints of many trade union leaders have done much in the past to prevent British organizations from achieving this goal.

Over the past two decades we have lived through an interesting experiment in abandoning the competitive principle – it is called the Common Agricultural Policy of the EEC. What was the result? Despite the endeavours of bureaucrats and Eurocrats there has been massive over-production of some agricultural products, a state which has been described as 'totally lunatic' by many observers. This would never have happened if the free flow of competition had been permitted. Economic absurdities are often the direct consequence of interference with the normal process of free trade.

In Britain the Conservative Government carried out a massive programme of privatization during the 1980s and argue that great benefits have followed. One thing is becoming clear: the mere transfer of ownership is not enough. Exchanging a public monopoly for a private monopoly will not do the trick. There must be real competition.

International competition

Imagine a country in which only one manufacturer built refrigerators and imports were prohibited. If someone wanted a refrigerator they could only buy from one product line. There is little doubt that products would only meet minimum standards for design and performance. Without a struggle for survival products of minimal efficiency are acceptable.

The Western industrial tradition is inherently competitive. Consider the ways in which personal computers have developed over recent years. We have seen an explosion of invention and initiative as competing computer manufacturers leapfrog one another in their attempt to reap the harvest. Only those who are most innovative, cost effective and quick off the mark survive. The consumer benefits through free choice. Another illustration of this principle is the vast difference between the quality of Russian and Western European cars. Freedom of choice requires that European motor manufacturers continually struggle to keep ahead. This is not true in the Eastern Block where the consumer suffers ill-designed and inefficient products. In the UK, the customer always invariably suffers when the state creates a monopoly. The success of the oil industry in profitably exploiting natural resources is an excellent case history of the benefits of competition. Oil companies compete with sharp claws: we all benefit.

Our belief is that the whole world benefits when competition operates freely. As the world becomes more and more one marketplace competitiveness within one nation is insufficient. An organization must be as good as similar concerns anywhere in the world; otherwise security is an illusion. Increasingly we live in a global economy and many economic and social problems are the direct result of the inability to compete on an international level. There can be no long-term solution to economic problems without a competitive edge.

People like competition, but only if they have a chance to win. Samantha Francis, daughter of Dave, is a student who said in conversation one day: 'I believe in competition. I've never wanted to win for the sake of winning, but I'm always happy to have someone to compete with. It brings the best out in me.' We could say it no better.

Summary

Core principles

- lack of competition damages people, organizations and nations
- competition is natural to human beings
- managers must learn more about the constructive use of competition as a motivator
- winning is a learnable set of skills
- not all competition is productive
- competition is not an end in itself, but a tool to be used
- competition between individuals is a powerful motivator but can be counter-productive
- managers should aim to make *all* employees into winners
- people gain from competing against standards
- accountants should be encouraged to provide competitive data
- intercompany competitiveness is crucial to overall effectiveness
- nations only succeed economically if they are internationally competitive.

Five steps to encourage competition

1 All employees should be assessed to evaluate how far their work comes up to the highest standards. Find ways of stimulating individuals to compete with themselves (like athletes). Institute regular (say, quarterly) self-improvement counselling sessions in which managers give each employee individual performance data and discuss how improvements can be made.
2 Teams tackling similar tasks are often motivated by competition. Identify teams where this would be useful and provide up-to-date information so that competitive performance can be judged. Brief

managers and supervisors to encourage competition. Reward winners.

3 Undertake a project to identify unconstructive uses of the competitive principle. Where destructive factors are uncovered these should be remedied by redefining objectives to make it clear who the real enemy is.

4 Ask the accounting function to re-examine the data it produces and report on how this can be better used to promote competition within the organization.

5 Establish a newsletter which gives up-to-date information on the performance of your organization compared to your competitors. Buy examples of their products and have them carefully analysed. Ensure that all of your employees know the strengths of the opposition.

Reference

1 *Guidelines for Directors 1982*, British Institute of Directors, London, p. 15.

14 Opportunism: Who dares wins

Despite the most brilliant planning it is inevitable that unexpected opportunities and threats will occur. Organizations cannot afford to ignore the unexpected. It is wiser to seek out new opportunities actively than allow others, more fleet of foot, to take the best chances. Often opportunities have to be seized quickly, even though this may involve risks. Successful managers are committed opportunists. They adopt the value: *who dares wins*.

The best way of holding a group of managers spellbound, like children listening to a ghost story, is to invite an outstandingly successful achiever to describe his or her commercial adventures. Managers are excited by tales of challenge and success which cause the adrenaline to flow. Primitive emotions are aroused, similar to those which our Stone Age ancestors probably experienced as they hunted the woolly mammoth.

The folk-lore of business is laden with tales of managers who saw an opportunity, pounced on it and turned an outside possibility into a commercial bonanza. This is opportunism and successful entrepreneurs are committed to acquiring the skills and willpower to seize and exploit opportunities.

Opportunists have a special view of the world: they perceive it as vastly complex, turbulent and continuously changing in unpredictable ways. 'Constant change is here to stay' and rewards those who dare to win. In volatile environments much can be planned, but there are always unpredictable elements which present rich pickings for opportunists who develop a zest for detecting, and rapidly exploiting, attractive possibilities.

Opportunism is more than a personal attribute: it becomes a cultural phenomenon within organizations and communities. For example, one of the primary reasons for the inadequate performance of British industry in recent decades was that its managers failed to be successful opportunists. In the eighteenth and nineteenth centuries the capacity of British industry to be creative exploiters was world renowned. One only has to look at a map dated before 1939 to see that one-third of the world was coloured red – the geographical extent of British influence. A decade or two later the UK was being described as a spent force drifting from economic mediocrity into terminal decline. We now detect signs of a renaissance of opportunism in management, as different economic policies reawaken latent opportunists. Opportunism is not simply creativity. Innovation itself abounds in Britain. A survey by Japan's Ministry for International Trade showed that over 55 per cent of significant inventions since World War Two have been British, which is more than any other country including the USA (22 per cent) and Japan (6 per cent). Britain's fault has been an inability to harvest successfully the rich field of opportunities and innovative ideas. A joke makes the point. It is said that a Russian pilot defected to Japan with the latest MiG fighter. Next day the Russian authorities asked to have their aeroplane back. The Japanese replied: 'Yes, of course, how many would you like?'

Adam Smith was correct when he said that people best help the public good by looking after themselves. An enterprise culture requires that people are rewarded for achievement rather than for having needs.

When we look around opportunism is everywhere. Perhaps the largest group of successful opportunists over the past twenty years are shopkeepers of Indian descent who saw that small retail businesses were missing much potential trade. They 'changed the rules' and captured business. Today few areas are without Asian-run stores which thrive because they offer a wanted service. Opportunities always exist, even in the least promising circumstances.

Individual inspiration is the first stage of opportunism, but there is more to it than that. The need must be real and the opportunist capable. Then a vision of a better future can be formed.

One of the most innovative thinkers on management of the postwar era, Edward de Bono, felt so strongly about exploiting opportunities that he wrote a book about it.[1] He begins by saying: 'An opportunity is as real an ingredient in business as raw material, labour or finance – but it only exists when you see it'. He goes on to tell a personal story of the time when he wanted to build a raised platform in his flat. He obtained various expensive quotations some of which involved a four-month delay. Then, inspiration! He invited an exhibition contractor to construct the platform which was done for half the conventional builder's cost within twenty-four hours. That was opportunism in action.

Opportunism is more than a management technique; it is a philosophy of life. We have a non-Jewish friend who asks for kosher food whenever he flies to the United States. Why? Kosher food is specially prepared and our friend gets an individual meal rather than a mass-produced concoction. Some years ago Gerald Francis realized that the other children in his school class became ravenous about midday. Quite unknown to his parents, he would buy a stock of sweets on his way to school. As the children reached the peak of hunger, Gerald sold his sweets for triple their cost. He frequently doubled his pocket money this way, even negotiating trade discounts with a shopkeeper for buying in quantity. In the summer he dealt in 'ice pops', keeping them cool in a special bag. Interestingly, this business only lasted for two years. Gerald had to seek new opportunities, saying 'as the kids grew up they got wiser, so I had to think of new ways to make money'.

Such illustrations abound. Tourists in Southern Italy can see a fine example of opportunism should they walk to the crater of Vesuvius. There is a small cafe just before the final lava-strewn path. As tourists see the steepness of the route they pass a lady watching for flimsy footwear. When a poorly shod tourist passes, the lady opportunist grasps the victim by the shoulder and says with a thick Italian accent, 'Shoes no good for walk. Hire shoes here only 1000 lira.' Many tourists are whisked into the cafe to emerge in sand shoes lined with plastic. The story is not over! The descent is dusty and as weary tourists pass the same cafe the lady stands by a collection of shoe brushes and a saucer for tips. She won our 'opportunist of the month' award!

Such stories have one thing in common: they are full of life, vitality or risk. Opportunism is a stance towards life which is inherently exciting. It is a fulfilment of a basic characteristic of the human spirit. No theory of motivation would be complete without it.

Individual opportunism

Opportunistic individuals have learned to think in particular ways, having taken a personal decision not to be swept along passively by life. The opportunist maintains an inquisitive sense of detached observation, watching events unfold which inevitably provide opportunities. These can then be exploited or avoided, depending on the wisdom of the opportunist and the potential payoff for success.

We can also learn about the nature of opportunism by examining the biographies of successful people from any walk of life. Outstanding careers are always a good fit between personal motives and that which the world has to offer. A career is each person's adventure and requires personal opportunism. The person who passively waits to be recognized is adopting a strategy with a high risk of failure. Opportunists take initiatives to make good things happen for themselves. They find new, often unexpected, possibilities which can be exploited.

Opportunism requires definite personal attributes which have been shown by Richard Boyatzis[2] to be key competencies in success at top management levels. Boyatzis has found in his research that three attributes are fundamental. He calls them 'Efficiency Orientation', 'Proactivity' and Diagnostic Use of Concepts' which are, in our opinion, the essence of opportunism. Don't be put off by the jargon. These ideas have real merit.

Firstly, Efficiency Orientation describes persons who are concerned to do things better; perhaps better than they have done previously, better than anyone else, or better than a standard. The individuals who have high Efficiency Orientation think in terms of standards, measurements and accomplishment. They are innovative and have highly developed skills in goal setting, planning and organizing. You can recognize them because they:

- set challenging but realistic targets
- take moderate risks
- measure their accomplishment
- have clearly describable 'inner' work standards
- state their standards clearly
- write plans and review them
- identify specific actions to be taken
- organize resources (money/time/people etc.)
- talk about 'return on investment', 'reward for effort', etc.
- watch for slippage of standards.

Proactivity describes a disposition towards taking action and accomplishing something. Activity is purposefully instigated. Proactive persons see themselves as the originators of actions in life. You can recognize them because they:

- see life and describe it in terms of taking action
- feel (and state) that they are the agents of change
- feel masters of their own lives
- feel in control of their own lives
- initiate events (communication, proposals, meetings etc.)
- possess information-seeking and problem-solving skills
- often take the first step
- take multiple steps to circumvent actual or potential obstacles
- develop relationships with providers of information
- accept responsibility for their own failures.

The third opportunistic competence is Diagnostic Use of Concepts. This describes an approach to thinking in which opportunists detect meaningful patterns in information. They organize, categorize and interpret events. Information is systematically tested against concepts. This way of thinking is deductive. Analytical and scientific approaches are valued. You can recognize people who are able to use concepts to diagnose situations because they:

- have models or theories to interpret events
- build models/theories to explain new events
- generalize from specific incidents to aid understanding
- ask for 'road maps' before they begin a project
- apply theories of influencing to persuade others to go along with their views
- perceive cues which tell them that a new set of concepts are necessary
- screen out irrelevant information
- categorize information in terms of whether it is critical, important or urgent.

These three 'competencies' give us a structured definition of opportunism. Although such attributes are difficult to teach, they can be learned. Developing individual opportunism is aided by the intentional application of the special thought processes and behaviours described. Our studies of opportunists have helped us identify eight distinctive characteristics that they seem to share:

1 They are aware of what is going on around them.
2 They know clearly what they like and what they want.

3   They seek to get the best available in any situation.
4   They do not allow themselves to get over-fatigued (tiredness blunts opportunism).
5   They learn to do two things at once (like exercising on a static cycle while watching television).
6   They practise seizing opportunities even when it doesn't really matter (getting the best table in each restaurant they enter).
7   They give themselves a reward whenever they successfully exploit an opportunity.
8   They mix with others who have developed the skills of identifying and seizing opportunities.

Opportunism requires an investment of thinking time. The manager must be willing to raise his or her head from immediate pre-occupations or short-term achievements to consider a possibly better future. Speculation is an essential indulgence for the opportunist. The opportunist is wary of being kept constantly busy as this diminishes time for thought. The effective opportunist will be willing to be a business heretic but will always try to reduce the risks of failure. This process was once well described to us as 'proactive conservatism', and is the essence of individual opportunism.

Organizational opportunism

Increasingly organizations are advocating opportunism as a way of life. In the past few years even the mighty IBM has reorganized itself to become less monolithic. Of course, organizations cannot be opportunistic themselves but they can create a climate in which individual opportunism flourishes. This requires that flexible structures must replace over-centralized decision making and red tape. The world is a volatile and changing place; the unpredictable will occur and opportunities arise when they are least expected. The opportunist organization is poised to take advantage of such serendipity. One chief executive wanted her company to be 'like a wild animal with its ears cocked and nose sniffing the air'. Organizational opportunism begins with well honed techniques for scanning the environment. The sagacious organization not only exploits accidents of fortune but also creates opportunities. A managing director told us: 'As the world becomes more competitive organizations must be opportunistic or they risk bankruptcy. That's it. Simple as that.'

Ironically some efforts to professionalize management have, unintentionally, undermined opportunism. Consider what happens in many large organizations when annual plans are prepared. The ground work for this highly analytical procedure begins months before presentation day. Environments are scanned, risks measured and options studiously evaluated. The macho image of managers requires a coherent and logical plan written to high intellectual standards. Senior managers often hire business school graduates to operate as planning specialists. Then months go by whilst plans are proposed, revised and re-presented. When finally agreed strategy documents are likely to have most opportunistic elements removed. One director told us with great feeling that 'rational long-term planning has destroyed the capacity to manage by the seats of our pants. The technocrats have the power and it's a dangerous situation.' Attempts to improve strategic planning systems to promote opportunism are slowly being introduced, and opportunist managers encourage trends away from worshipping only the gods of rationality and predictability.

In addition to the anti-opportunistic bias of many corporate planning systems there is another potential barrier to effective corporate opportunism. Those promoted to powerful roles often gain their high status through being excellent underlings. Such people are masters of their specializations. They administer supremely well, devise superb systems, but are naturally inclined towards safety and continuity. In our experience, successful organizations try to counter built-in risk avoidance by working to give individuals with entrepreneurial flair room to breathe. This builds a dynamic into top management, as opportunistic people dare to win.

Inspired change is rarely accomplished from conventional assumptions. One person needs a vision of a better future and the will power to push through innovative ideas. This individual is a product champion. The word 'champion' is well chosen. It means 'one who fights for any cause. One who has defeated all opponents in any trial of strength or skill, and is open to contend with any new competitor' (*Shorter Oxford Dictionary*). Opportunism is a characteristic of individual champions, and systems should permit champions to emerge. This is seen in the continuing upsurge of small businesses, which have none of the wealth of larger well established concerns, but are fuelled by individuals with the will power and the preparedness to seize an opportunity.

Large organizations must work hard to avoid acquiring an inertia which inhibits opportunism. Today enterprises cannot afford to wait for individuals to champion bright ideas – top management must structure opportunism. Historically many organizations contain new ideas which are killed off by uninterested middle-management. Many senior managers are rewarded for maintaining control and limiting waste and, whilst this is essential, the organization must avoid eliminating opportunism because it is untidy.

Re-orienting an organization towards a greater appreciation of economic factors is possible. Companies like the American Dow Chemical group have instituted a deliberate policy to rebuild a corporate culture based on commercial criteria. Steps that the Dow company undertook include:

- asking the question in performance reviews: 'What have you done that's new?'
- putting an evangelistic but practical top manager in charge of 'debureaucratizing'
- being prepared to act unconventionally
- forming a high-level action group to progress practical innovation
- ensuring that new ideas are identified by a 'technological gate-keeper'
- telling, selling and persuading people that changes are essential by presenting well argued cases
- convincing managers that if they are 'not part of the solution they are part of the problem'
- truthfully answering questions from sceptics in order to build credibility
- reorganizing to make new resources available for development
- bringing development specialists close to the marketplace
- removing excessive hierarchies to speed decision making
- identifying and unblocking communication blockages
- having an independently funded entrepreneurial department
- providing facilities to incubate new projects
- making 'beachhead acquisitions' to give footholds in new technologies
- fighting the tendency to overwhelm new acquisitions by bureaucracy.

Edward de Bono suggests that companies should structure opportunity seeking by instituting regular opportunity audits. Each executive is encouraged regularly to examine his or her 'opportunity space'. At the corporate level Opportunity Teams co-ordinate the search for promising new ideas. de Bono points out that large company executives are trained to solve problems as they arise rather than seize opportunities. This is an 'opportunity negative structure'. He echoes our own theme when he writes: 'The words 'opportunity' and 'opportunist' have had connotations. They suggest a hovering vulture rather than a hovering eagle . . . The opposite of opportunity-seeking is not stability or conservatism, it is stagnation and atrophy.'

An interesting illustration of the vital importance of organizational opportunism is shown by the fortunes of the British telecommunications industry. For many years their products were dictated by a conventional Post Office. Although standards were rigorous the level of innovation was low. In the late 1970s liberalization opened doors to radical new products. Equipment from foreign suppliers began to compete with British manufacturers. This forced a revolution in the organization of telecommunication equipment companies who, for the first time, had to establish marketing departments and study consumers. It became imperative that a creative, flexible and consumer-oriented philosophy permeated from top to bottom. One of the authors was privileged to be a consultant to a telecommunication equipment manufacturer and watched the creaks and groans as a total organization changed its structure, culture and technology from old-style bureaucracy to emerge bursting with opportunism.

Organizational opportunism is correctly described as entrepreneurial. The original meaning of the word entrepreneur is 'a person who stages dramas'. Later the word became associated with commercial opportunists who seize possibilities which others fail to perceive or exploit. The entrepreneur is most definitely not an obedient functionary and so has difficulty fitting into centralized bureaucracies. Entrepreneurship tends to be better developed in small businesses; the market stall holder or scrap metal merchant is more likely to be a highly skilled opportunist than a system-bound middle manager in a large organization.

Successful organizational opportunism can be encouraged by:

- wholehearted top management commitment to successful innovation
- a culture which encourages opportunism by showing that venturesomeness is valued
- training for managers in skills of managing innovation

- creating mixed teams of developers and implementors to exploit ideas
- offering tangible rewards and power to acknowledged innovators
- allowing product champions room to grow
- supporting entrepreneurial 'nurseries' which allow risky but limited projects to flourish for a time
- 'mentoring' by experienced opportunists to transfer their attitudes and skills to more junior talent
- devising imaginative suggestion schemes which collect ideas from large numbers of people
- providing mechanisms which carefully evaluate ideas
- identifying and exploiting sources of venture finance which assist opportunistic projects to get off the ground
- maintaining overall commercial strength so enabling resources to be available for entrepreneurial ventures
- becoming highly skilled at evaluating potential markets for new ideas
- being prepared to tolerate unconventional behaviour from successful opportunists.

Opportunism is a primary duty of management. The structure of organizations means that those at the top are in an extraordinarily privileged position. Only they can exploit greater opportunities. Those working in subordinate roles are dependent on the opportunism of top managers. Managers, therefore, should accept that they have a moral obligation to be opportunistic. Only by seeking possible avenues for success or profit can they provide the positive leadership that their employees properly demand. In this context employee or trade union pressure can provide a useful stimulus. One electrical manufacturer we know decided to abandon an obsolete product and make 300 people redundant. The trade union pushed managers by asking: 'What have you done to find other products to replace the redundant line?' Management recognized that it had not fully considered the opportunities and was encouraged to make a full study. The result was a range of new products which actually increased employment and business profitability. Opportunism thrives when we are 'a little bit hungry'.

Summary

Core principles

- the world can never be totally planned: opportunities always occur

- opportunism is more than a philosophy of management: it is a way of life
- many individuals can develop opportunistic attitudes and skills but are not encouraged to do so in bureaucracies
- opportunism needs a framework of principles or it can become a tool for immoral exploitation
- organizations can change their structures and cultures to encourage opportunists
- entrepreneurial skills are most naturally developed in small enterprises
- rigid strategic planning procedures often inhibit opportunism
- some (but not all) top managers should be proven opportunists
- successful opportunists should be rewarded, both with recognition and material rewards
- unsuccessful opportunists should also be rewarded, with recognition and guidance (at least they tried!)
- it is essential to look outward at the environment (it is too easy to put all your effort into managing the status quo)
- large companies should embrace a deliberate policy of encouraging opportunism
- pressure groups can be used to sharpen opportunistic thinking.

Five steps to encourage opportunism

1 Encourage individual opportunist skills through training programmes which develop entrepreneurial competence. Ensure that these encourage self-awareness and put people into situations in which real opportunities exist. Tell your training department to prepare such a programme. (Use de Bono's book on opportunities as a basis.)

2 Review organization procedures, structures and systems to see whether potential opportunities are being lost through a surfeit of red tape.[3] Develop an experimental 'fast track' to get ideas into top decision-making teams quickly. Set up a multidisciplinary task group to advise on how this can be accomplished.

3 Search for practical ways to reward opportunism at every level from director to shopfloor employees. Recognition, feedback and encouragement should be used in addition to monetary gain. Tell your personnel director to review your reward policy with this in mind.

4 Look ahead for five to ten years in as much detail as possible.
   (Institutes like the Business School Forecasting Centres can help.)
   Conduct a detailed analysis of the trends which are likely to affect
   your markets and technology? Hold senior management teach-ins
   to discuss potential opportunities. Establish a structure of 'options
   teams' to explore opportunities. Progress many ideas at the same
   time. Ensure that the top team is kept in contact with the findings.
5 Set up 'opportunity' panels with people from your organization and
   present or potential customers. Organize periodic discussions, trials
   of new products and idea exchange sessions. Some companies
   estimate that 60 per cent of good ideas come this way. Ensure that
   the marketing director has this as an objective.

References

1 Edward de Bono, *Opportunities*, Penguin, Harmondsworth, 1980.
2 Richard Boyatzis, *The Competent Manager: a Model for Effective
   Performance*, Wiley, 1982.
3 Mike Woodcock and Dave Francis, *Unblocking Your Organization*, Gower, Aldershot, 1990.

Index